970.3 Sc84k 1992
Scott, Lalla
Karnee
HAY LIBRARY
WESTERN WYOMING COMMUNITY COLLEGE

DISCARDED

KARNEE

A PAIUTE NARRATIVE

D0746183

Vintage West Series

Sagebrush Trilogy: Idah Meacham Strobridge
and Her Works
by Idah Meacham Strobridge, 1904, 1907, 1909

Lady in Boomtown: Miners and Manners
on the Nevada Frontier
by Mrs. Hugh Brown, 1968

The WPA Guide to 1930s Nevada
by the Nevada Writers' Project of the WPA, 1940

A Kid on the Comstock: Reminiscences of a
Virginia City Childhood
by John Taylor Waldorf, 1970

The Story of the Mine
by Charles Howard Shinn, 1896

Will James: The Last Cowboy Legend
by Anthony Amaral, 1980

Karnee: A Paiute Narrative
by Lalla Scott, 1966

KARNEE

A PAIUTE NARRATIVE

by
LALLA SCOTT
annotated by
CHARLES R. CRAIG

University of Nevada Press
Reno • Las Vegas • London

VINTAGE WEST SERIES EDITOR:
ROBERT E. BLESSE

The paper used in this book meets the requirements of
American National Standard for Information Sciences—
Permanence of Paper for Printed Library Materials,
ANSI Z39.48-1984.

Library of Congress Cataloging-in-Publication Data
Scott, Lalla, 1894–1981.
Karnee : a Paiute narrative / by Lalla Scott.
p.   cm. — (Vintage West series)
Originally published: Reno : University of Nevada Press, 1966.
Includes bibliographical references.
ISBN 0-87417-189-X (pbk. : alk. paper)
1. Lowry, Annie.   2. Sau-tau-nee.   3. Paiute Indians—
Biography.   4. Paiute Indians—Mixed descent.   5. Paiute
Indians—History.   I. Title.
E99.P2L697   1992
979.3'53—dc20
[B]
92-7571
CIP

University of Nevada Press, Reno, Nevada 89557 USA
Copyright © 1966 by University of Nevada Press
All rights reserved
Book design by William H. Snyder
Cover design by Mary Mendell
Printed in the United States of America
2   4   6   8   9   7   5   3   1

To my devoted husband,
"Scotty, the Assayer" (A. H. Scott),
who declares he did not help
write this book.

PREFACE

Anthropological literature is rich in autobiographical accounts of American Indians* and in these the reader can often perceive, through the narrow individual experience which is necessarily subjective, examples of some of the forms and values peculiar to the culture of the author. Biographies are a quite different sort of document since they aim at being objective in telling the story of a person's life as it proceeded in the milieu of a particular culture. The material for the biography of Annie Lowry has been gathered and is presented without embellishment by Mrs. Scott, who has been my friend for forty years. Mrs. Scott is not and does not pretend to be an ethnographer, and Annie Lowry's life history is not intended to be an anthropological document although a considerable amount of substantive ethnological fact occurs in the account. Annie's (I can be pardoned for using her first name for she too was my friend) contributions to formal ethnography are contained in Robert H. Lowie's *Notes on Shoshonean Ethnography* and Omer Stewart's culture element survey of the Northern Paiute. I mention this to affirm that these eminent students of American Indian

* For a discussion of these as anthropological documents see A. L. Kroeber, *The Nature of Culture* University of Chicago Press, 1951, (pp. 233–243, 320–326, 423).

culture considered her to be a reliable authority on Paiute culture. Her biography, as presented here through Mrs. Scott's efforts, is the unadorned and factual recital of a "half-blood," the peculiar institution of the advancing western frontier of America. Here is the dilemma of a person who is the biological product of two members of opposing social groups. She is beset with the difficulties of trying to become a Caucasian, as her father demanded, because she is considered by the whites as an Indian. But the struggle was not worth the effort, there being no real support for it from either parent, so Annie made the decision to take the easier, and probably less emotionally disruptive, alternative of joining forces with her mother. But by doing this, and even after her two marriages (with Sanny and John Pascal), she was never wholly Indian since she was fully literate and conscious of her descent.

Think, if you will, of yourself having to make such a choice as she was forced to make. Few white Americans have been confronted with the agonizing immediate decision of which of two worlds to live in. Annie's solution was one which was successful if we are to judge by her character and her ability to live in the two worlds. It would be an error to try to make Annie the Paiute heroine, for she was not. She was an individual like the rest of us, and it is precisely because of this that every reader will understand the human message that her story bears.

Berkeley, California   ROBERT F. HEIZER
October, 1965

ACKNOWLEDGMENTS

As it is impossible to thank by name the scores of people who, over the years, gave data for this book, I would like all to feel they had a part in its making. Although deceased, I wish to express my appreciation to two Pershing County teachers, Helen Fancher and Emma Coppin, whose interest and criticism encouraged me to submit "Karnee" for publication.

My grateful thanks to:

Donald Bowers, whose encouragement led me, in 1961, to write the biography of Annie Lowry.

Edna Van Reed, typist, whose persistence and talent enabled me to finish the manuscript; and Betty Armstrong, for preliminary editing.

Eva Wasson Pancho and Mabel Summerfield, who authenticated many of the incidents related to me by their mother.

Charles R. Craig, for annotation and commentary.

LALLA SCOTT

CONTENTS

INTRODUCTION

The substance of this story was told by a half-breed Indian woman named Annie Lowry, who was born nearly one hundred years ago and lived out her life in the vicinity of Lovelock, Nevada. During the summer of 1936, she met Lalla Scott, also of Lovelock, who was then doing research for the Pershing County Writers' Project (under the Work Projects Administration). Over a period of several months, Annie told what she knew of her mother's life, and the notes taken by Mrs. Scott at that time formed the basis for the following narrative.

The manuscript records local Indian history and lore, as Annie had heard these from her mother and the older Indians, and provides something of a biography of both Annie and her mother, Sau-tau-nee, with later history and lore interspersed by Mrs. Scott.

Mrs. Scott had heard of Annie through a mutual friend, Mr. John T. Reid, and her name had been suggested at the WPA office as a source for information on aspects of local history and culture. On June 2, 1936, Mrs. Scott walked to Annie's house in the Indian colony, introduced herself, and explained why she had come. She was invited in, and Annie agreed to act as her informant. The first interviews were rather specific. Annie described the building of an Indian hut, or demonstrated the method by which the women winnowed the grass seed which had been their food in the old days. She spoke good English and loved to talk, and Mrs. Scott took notes as quickly and accurately as she could. Some of these notes were condensed, typed, and sent to the Writers' Project. Others remained as fairly accurate transcriptions of the original telling. During the summer after the Writers' Project had closed, Mrs. Scott returned to Annie's house and asked her to tell all she knew of how the Indians lived before the white men came. The relationship between Mrs. Scott and Annie grew more personal, and though Mrs. Scott still took notes of their conversations, the visits became social rather than formal. At some point, Annie began to talk about her mother's childhood, then of her own, and then of her adult life.

It was not until the Writers' Project was closed that Mrs. Scott conceived the idea of coordinating her material into a sustained narrative. She obtained permission from her supervisor to use the material gathered for the WPA, and some portions of the present text remain in substantially the same form as the reports prepared in 1936, but the biographical material into which they were incorporated represents her own efforts, independent of the Writers' Project. The author began writing again in January of 1961, and the book was finished in August of that year. In its lengthened form, it was sent to the University of Nevada Press, where the publications board recommended that it be annotated and published as a document containing significant source material.

Structurally, the book falls into two parts: that portion leading up to Sau-tau-nee's marriage, and that in which Annie tells the story of her own life. In the first portion the general tone is subjective; action is either dramatized or told in retrospect through the device of the flashback. The first person appears occasionally, but it is never sustained. In contrast, the last chapters are quite consistent in their point of view and are considerably more objective and unified. The change in style may be attributed to a lapse of seven years between the writing of the first part and the second, and a corresponding shift in the author's intentions and attitude toward her material.

Those chapters which deal with Sau-tau-nee's early years were not, as the first chapter suggests, written to be simply the story of an Indian girl as told by her daughter. It was intended to tell the story of the Paiutes as well, describing their history, legends, beliefs, and customs, and their early encounters with white civilization. The broad outlines of Sau-tau-nee's early life were depicted accurately enough, but they were also made to serve as a framework which was then supplemented with passages containing lore, historical background material, and the story of Cap John. Most of the material was taken from the notes made by the author at the time of her interviews with Annie Lowry, but some was obtained from Annie's daughters or other Indians. Some, pertaining to the exploration of the West, was adapted from published works. Thus, in the first portion of the manuscript we have a composite text consisting of authentic and verifiable material linked together into the life story of a real person—Sau-tau-nee. The second portion of the book is also a composite text, but only to a degree. Here, the author worked almost directly from her notes, transcribing them with a minimum of revision. The first person point of view is retained, and those passages consisting of nonbiographical material fit naturally into Annie's story of her own life. Here, too, there is some interloping matter, usually material originating from local Indians, but these instances are few and brief. As a whole, the story of Annie's life is detailed, unified, and realistic.

Aside from its interest as a personal chronicle, much of

the value of this manuscript depends upon the reliability of the author's sources, the authenticity of the anthropological material presented, and the accuracy of its transmission. Because the manuscript, by reason of its nature, does not consistently and explicitly provide such information, it has seemed necessary to provide notes which will identify the author's sources whenever significant, and to comment upon the accuracy of the material and the manner in which it has been set down. Aside from several instances which involve questions of accuracy, the annotator has not attempted to trace the history of individual passages. Considerable attention has also been given to ethnological and historical sources other than those used by the author. The annotator has referred to published studies of the Indians of the Great Basin, especially those of the Lovelock area, and the information given in the following pages has been checked against the body of information established by others. As Annie Lowry has found her way into several formal ethnological surveys, it has been possible in several instances to compare her statements as given here to those given elsewhere. Cap John's influence in the affairs of northwestern Nevada is also confirmed by a number of references in sources dealing with the area. Other notes, such as those clarifying references to local geographical features or defining such Indian terms not immediately clear in the text, are offered as aids to the reader's understanding.

In no instance has any alteration changed the original meaning or substance of the narrative, and all revisions were made in accordance with the wishes expressed by Mrs. Scott.

Reno, Nevada　　　　　　　　　　　　CHARLES R. CRAIG
October, 1965

1

PRELUDE

MOST Paiute Indians have long memories, and some of them are gifted story tellers, or have talent for drawing and painting. But they are a secretive people, never confiding their ideas and beliefs to anyone but their family, passing traditions from one generation to another. Because of this reticence, much of the Indian history and culture has been lost. I, too, feel timid about talking to outsiders, but as the young people of our tribe are not even interested in these stories that have been handed down through the generations, I feel that I should tell them to someone who will record them for future reference.

The young people of today find it more to their liking to take up with the white man's ways. They seem to forget anything pertaining to their heritage. My children and grandchildren have never listened to my stories about our history as they were always too busy or found something else to occupy their minds. The only one who showed the least bit of interest was Wilbur Wasson, one of the sons of my daughter, Eva. Wilbur used to stay with me, and sometimes he would ask me to tell him stories about the Paiute Indians, just as the white children are always asking for fairy tales. In relating these events, I feel as if my mother were a girl of whom I had read, and as if my ancestors belonged to another group of people who have nothing to do with the Paiutes surrounding me in this village.

We have learned, as a race, very little from the white people that has been helpful. On the other hand, the Paiutes have easily absorbed the bad habits of the people my father used to call "poor white trash."[1] The ideas of right and wrong of the ancient people were stricter in the old times than they are today. It hurts me to see the young people so changed from the time when one husband was all a woman was allowed to have in her lifetime to now, when they are running wild, staying out at night, drinking, and smoking.[2] I believe whiskey has been the downfall of not only the Paiutes, but of all the Indians of the West. There is no such thing as an Indian carrying his liquor "like a gentleman." When under the influence of drink, the Indian of the present time is much wilder than he was in the days gone by when he dressed in skins and feathers and went out to kill the white man who had taken his land and his homes. Lest I grow bitter, I shall go ahead with my story.

I am a half-breed. That means I live on the fringe of two races. My white friends think I am just a plain old Paiute, while the Indians say I think I am better than they because my father was a white man. When the time came to make a choice between the Indians and the white race, I made up my mind to be an Indian. At that time I felt resentful toward my white father because he was not fair to my mother. I was determined that no white man would ever make me suffer as Jerome Lowry, my father, a white man, made my little Indian mother suffer. I know I was right to choose the Indians for my people because I loved them more. Anything Indian I learned quickly, but to the white teaching my mind was closed.

2
CAP JOHN'S FATHER'S DREAM

PEOPLE in Lovelock remember my mother by the name of Susie. They remember her as a one-eyed Indian squaw who kept my father from marrying one of their women.[3] I remember her as Sau-tau-nee, which means Willow Blossom.

When Cap John's father's dream came true, Sau-tau-nee was just a little girl, nearly running her little legs off trying to keep up with the big, long-legged Indians who set the pace for the women and children. She was big enough to know of that old medicine man's dream, when one day word went out that the dream had really come true. Now, Cap John's father was a very wise man who knew many things that he never confided to a mortal soul, but he did tell the dream, not only to his immediate family, but to all the tribe so everyone knew, from the old men down to little girls like Sua-tau-nee. At this time no Paiute had seen a horse or a burro.[4] When they wanted to go somewhere they walked or swam. They had never seen men with skin different from their own, and yet Cap John's father had dreamed of these things and had told the dream many times around the campfire.

He dreamed that early one morning two women were in an open space, fanning chaff from the seed which they were preparing to grind for mush. While they were fan-

3

ning, they looked up and beheld a strange apparition. There, walking toward them, were two men. They were men with white skin and white eyes, with hair on their faces, leading two strange creatures with big ears and wall eyes.[5] He dreamed that the women screamed and threw down their yattahs[6] and ran away. He dreamed that he was not afraid, so he walked to meet them. He talked to them in his language which they did not seem to understand. They spoke some strange jargon and then turned and went away.

Cap John's father's dream had become so familiar to the Paiutes that when a group of them heard a woman scream and saw the familiar signal to move, they knew at once that they must get across the water to safety as fast as they could. They were camping at this time on the east side of what was later known as Humboldt Lake.[7] They thought if they could get to the opposite side they would be safe, so sometimes they waded and sometimes they swam. They were fleeing for their lives. The braves stuck eagle feathers into their hair over their ears. They believed that these feathers made otters of men and that they could swim as long as there was water.[8] The otter men were kind to the fat old women and to the little girls who had not learned to swim. They helped Sau-tau-nee, but she wished she could be a tall, slim, brave otter man with eagle feathers over her ears.

So frightened were these Paiute Indians at the white man's first appearance in the Big Meadows of the Humboldt River that they did not stop to rest until they had reached the Granite Point, a long way from the fright of the morning.[9] Here was dry ground. The women gathered seeds and ground them between rocks to make meal. They pulled pliable green tules,[10] using them to thatch the karnee[11] and, after cutting off about two feet nearest the root, for fuel. This delicious morsel, the root, was saved for food. After they had rested and eaten their scant food they began to compare the real happening of the morning with Cap John's father's unusual dream, noting any discrepancies between the dream and the real happening. From this time on, until years after his death, the mystical powers of Cap John's father became a legend.

The old man had dreamed there would be two women fanning chaff from seed with a yattah, which is a fan-shaped basket. There was really only one woman but she had screamed loud enough for two, being heard in the farthest karnee. The woman who had seen the horrible sight was asked to relate her experience. Over and over again she told how she was winnowing the pigweed and heard strange talk. She looked up to see two men with hair on their faces, leading two big animals that had ears like jack rabbits, long faces, and very big eyes. She had not tried to listen to what the men said; she only knew that Cap John's father's dream had come true. She had thrown her yattah to the ground, scattering seed in all directions, while she let out one big scream and ran to the karnee to help send out the signal for everyone to move. Cap John said he would vouch for the scream because he had heard it. When he unrolled himself from the deer hide to see what had happened, he saw the rear end of two animals that looked more like the hind parts of deer than jack rabbits. But they were not moving like deer, nor antelope, nor mountain sheep. The walk was too different and they were brown in color. So the Paiutes argued back and forth, talking about the strange things seen in the early morning.

Cap John was young and brave. He wished the woman

had not screamed so loud. Maybe he could have made talk with these strange animals or with the men who had hair on their faces. He was all for going back to see if any more such strange creatures came down the trail. The other men, lacking Cap John's courage, thought it was not safe for the women and children to be near such terrible danger. Sau-tau-nee gave a delighted shiver, wishing she could have seen the long-eared, bald-faced animals, but most of all she wished she had been big enough to accompany Cap John back to see what really happened to the strange creatures.

A few days later, other Indians came with the news that these two strange men with hair on their faces had met a hunting party near what is known as the Forty Mile Desert.[12] The Paiute braves, knowing it was not right for men to be so different from themselves, stoned them to death. They took their clothes, each one a garment, and tried them on. The big jack rabbits they killed and cut up for meat, intending to keep the skins for blankets. But when they came into camp, the people fought so much over the clothing and the skins that they had to be torn into small pieces so everyone could have a souvenir. Everybody had something now, and nobody had anything. When Sau-tau-nee saw these things she was more sorry than ever that she had not seen the strange clothing before it had been torn into fragments.

3

DISCOVERY OF THE HUMBOLDT RIVER

A S the white men came in ever increasing numbers, the Indians continued to be afraid and to run and hide when they received the signal that a caravan was coming. During the spring and summer they fled over Ragged Top to the beautiful Pyramid Lake where trout were so plentiful.[13] In autumn they would rush early to their winter camping grounds in the Pine Nut Range[14] or to Table Mountain.[15] The Indian men were so frightened and set such a fast pace that the women with babies on their backs and little ones too small to walk fast could not keep up and would almost die of hurry and fright. Sometimes they would stop long enough to bury the children—all but their heads, which they covered with sage and rabbit brush. The poor women then raced to catch up with the braves. Late in the evening someone would venture back and dig up the children. Sarah Winnemucca used to tell of being buried in this fashion with her brother when they were children in Muddlebury Canyon.[16]

As time passed, the Indians noted the white men were killing off the already fast-disappearing antelope, deer, and mountain sheep that furnished their livelihood. As these animals became scarce, the Paiutes depended more and more upon the beaver for both food and clothing.[17] They caught many beaver at the Big Dam at the end of what is now Ruddle's ranch. The beaver had built this dam one year when the river was running to mud. It was three feet wide and about fifty feet long and was five feet high in most places. It was built much better than the ranchers who came later could build. Any of the old timers can tell about the Big Dam, for it was used until a few years ago. The Indians fished from the dam, and each season when they had caught enough prime beaver, they moved to Table Mountain for the winter.

Now the trappers were taking not only all the beaver in sight, but were gutting the streams that flowed into the river. The trappers acted as though they owned the Humboldt River. A man named Ogden[18] claimed he discovered it and named it the "Unknown River." My people caught beaver in the "Unknown River" before Columbus discovered America.

Joe Paul[19] was the first white man known to have been buried in Nevada. His grave was marked and later became a landmark for the Paiutes. When they were camping in the vicinity of what is now Mill City, they would make it a point to visit the grave. My mother said they would come to Paul's grave every year for their rendezvous of several days. These meetings were similar to the picnics and camp meetings of the white people. To the Indians, a meeting at the grave with the headboard was like the gathering at a monument or shrine. I can show where the grave is, as my mother showed it to me. She used to go there every year to meet friends from the other bands of Paiutes.[20] For forty years after Paul's death, the trappers called the Humboldt River "Paul's River." During the same time, the explorers called it "Ogden's River."

4

THE BATTLE OF THE LAKES

*C*AP JOHN had never been as afraid of the strange white man as were his brother tribesmen. Nor did he have the terrible hate for them that seemed to burn in the others. When he learned that Ogden had taken an Indian wife and that Joe Paul had died and was buried at Mill City, his fear of the whites completely vanished. He figured they must be human, and he wanted to be friends with them, even if they did grow hair on their faces and have light eyes which his father had said were white. The Indians of those days did not have hair on their faces nor on their bodies. He kept saying to himself and to all who listened, "My father was not afraid of these people. In his dream he talked to them even if they did not understand."

"No, they have killed our animals. They have taken our food," he was told.

"Even so, we have nothing to lose and all to gain by being friendly," said Cap John.

"Look at what they have done to the beaver, no more warmth from those fine skins," they argued. "The antelope, the finest food ever sent by the Big Man—all gone."

At first nobody agreed, but slowly Cap John evolved a plan to interest the old men who could not hunt and the young men who had no responsibility for getting food. Up and down the river, around the Humboldt and Carson sinks, went Cap John, always persuading and always telling the Paiutes the advantage of friendship with the white men who were now coming down the Humboldt Trail. At last it was agreed that at a signal each band of Paiutes would send some of its young men to meet and greet the next band of white men that came down the river.

The Paiutes had long since developed a signal system by which they could send messages to the furthermost band of the tribe within a few hours. Several days after this agreement the signal came. Within a few hours, young braves from all Paiute bands up and down the river, on the Sink, and from Pyramid Lake began wending their way to the meeting place in the hills above what is now called the Humboldt Sink. From this vantage point they could keep hidden and yet observe the movements of the white caravan. They had planned to reach the meeting place the day before their visit was to take place.

It was a thrilling adventure, as many of the young men had never been away overnight from their relatives. They passed the time playing games and telling stories. They laughed and pretended they would not be afraid of the strange creatures they were expecting to meet. They bragged about how they would boldly take the queer head-pieces from the white men and try them on. Much time was spent in dressing for the occasion. Wearing only a few skins which they used for breechcloths, they covered their bodies with the brightest and most startling designs. Circles, half-moons, triangles, wedges, and dots were painted in crude but colorful designs. The general appearance was extremely gruesome. Waves of excitement ran through the crowd of two hundred young Paiutes as they boldly marched toward the white man's camp.

The Shoshones, who lived above what is now Elko, had tormented the Walker-Bonneville trappers every step of the way from the northern mountains to Mill City.[21] They had stolen their food and traps, frightened their horses, and created all sorts of destruction. For many days his men had wanted to fight these Indians, but Walker, a peace-loving man, had refused to let them do anything about their losses. Just the day before, a group of fifty Shoshones appeared, making signs that they wanted to come into camp. In order to stop them, Walker's men put on a shooting exhibition. They stretched a beaver skin and shot it full of holes. Instead of frightening the Shoshones, this trick only made them laugh. Changing targets, the white men aimed at the ducks on the river, and when the ducks fell over, the Indians ran for their lives.

The trappers were highly pleased, but the exhibition had been so simple that they thought perhaps the Indians might return. They could not afford to lose more traps or horses. Because the men were so nervous the next morning, Walker gave orders to break camp before they had had enough rest. All day, as they marched, the men saw eyes peering at them from the brush on the river and caught glimpses of human forms slipping from boulder to boulder in the Humboldt Range.

They had just pitched camp at the south end of the Humboldt Sink when they saw a troop of Indians coming toward them. With their tempers at fever pitch, they were certain that it was the Indians of yesterday's experience. These, of course, were young Paiutes hurrying from all directions to connect with Cap John.

The oncoming band of two hundred Paiute braves confirmed the fears of Walker's men. The smiling, prancing, high-stepping Paiutes looked to Walker and his men like a reinforced band of the restless Indians who had so shamelessly run the day before. Thinking these were the Shoshones come to drive them away, the long-suffering Walker gave orders to his men to prepare for battle. The trappers hastily made a barricade of their tents and baggage two hundred feet from the camp. The men were divided, and those with guns were sent out to stop the savages before they reached the camp.

Instead of halting when they saw the men pointing their guns, the Paiutes, with smiles on their painted faces, lifted their prancing feet higher and came forward. At the sound of the guns, the reception party scattered and fell to the ground. They had never heard gunshot, and they thought it was a clap of thunder.

After a few volleys, the Paiutes knew the white men were fighting with deadly weapons and did not want to be friends. Cap John had wronged them by persuading them to make overtures to strangers. They were hurt, they were angered, and they were afraid as they ran for their lives. Thirty-nine of the finest young Paiutes were killed in what history calls the "Battle of the Lakes." The first friendly overtures made by the Paiutes turned out to be a terrible tragedy. This marked the beginning of ill feeling and warfare between the two races.[22]

5

CAP JOHN

AFTER the "Battle of the Lakes," Cap John[23] did not return to his own band of Paiutes for many moons. He never talked freely about where he went or what he did during those seasons, but when he came back he could speak English and had become an expert guide. In the season when the Paiutes were fishing on Pyramid Lake, Cap John was one of the two Indians who came to offer salmon and trout to an exploration party camping on the lake.[24] After eating, the leader, whose name was Captain John Frémont, said he had never tasted such good fish. He talked to Cap John about the fish and asked him about the surrounding country. He found that Cap John knew all the trails and asked him to guide his party to what is now known as Walker Lake. This was Captain Frémont's second expedition.[25] This party had divided near Humboldt House. Frémont, Kit Carson, and eight other men had gone across by Rabbit Hole to Pyramid Lake. The rest of the expedition, under the leadership of Captain Joseph Walker, had kept to the Humboldt Trail. The two parties had arranged to meet at Walker Lake. So it was ten years after the "Battle of the Lakes" that Cap John and Walker met again.[26]

All the rest of Cap John's life he remembered the trip with the great Frémont, and to his dying day he kept the letter, written in Frémont's own hand, telling all who might read that Cap John was a fair and honest and upright Indian, and asking the reader to lend a kindly hand if need be to the man who had served his government as a guide over a dangerous pass. He gave him money, too. But best of all, he, Captain Frémont of the topographical engineers, presented to the Indian, Cap John, a beautiful flag of the United States.[27]

With the money, the precious letter, and his beautiful American flag, Cap John came back to the river which Frémont had told him should be called the Humboldt. Frémont had named it again, this time for a German scientist, Count Alexander von Humboldt, who was an explorer but who never came near the Humboldt River named for him. Many caravans and emigrant trains were now coming down the Humboldt Trail and Cap John set up a station for them in the Big Meadows on the place where Carpenter's ranch stands.[28] Here the weary travelers and their animals could rest overnight or for a few days before crossing the Forty Mile Desert which was already known for the number of dead men and animals along its route. Cap John sold or traded, for useful or ornamental articles, wild hay and fresh game or jerked venison. A variation from the monotonous diet of the long road behind them was welcome.[29]

Word went out that the finest hay in the world could be bought at Cap John's emigrant station. His wives and their parents, sisters, and brothers were a great help in cutting the wild hay or guarding the emigrants while they slept. When he took a new wife, Cap John courted her in Paiute fashion, but after he was married things were changed. Instead of going to live with his wife at her parents', as was the custom of his people, be brought her to his emigrant station to help gather hay for the animals of the people passing by. Not to be outdone, the parents of the bride came to the station and demanded that Cap John live with them. Cap John pretended to be angry at first, but his eye for business told him that the old men and women about his place added to the interest of the emigrants, and more and more the travelers stopped overnight on their long trek to the west.

Cap John made exorbitant charges for this wonderful, sweet, wild hay and the customer usually paid without complaint. If, however, a complaint was made, Cap John would put on a hurt expression with a sort of "me don't understand" shake of the head, take out the letter of good will penned by the great Frémont, and present it to be read. If the dissatisfied customer was not interested, or could not read, Cap John brought himself to an erect position, held the paper before his eyes, pretending to read, and recited from memory every word written on the page. He now considered his character had been established, and to the first price named he added a slight charge for the inconvenience of showing the priceless manuscript.[30]

Regulations of the tribe allowed two or three wives. Cap John already had three and said he would take five or six, adding one every year as he prospered.[31] Of what use were goods and money but to be given away? Therefore, why not give to one's own and have lots of people living around? Cap John was sure his wealth would continue to increase.

Cap John's wives liked him. He beat them occasionally, but he kept them living in an interesting place, and they had more ornaments than other men's women.[32] It was pleasant to gather the sweet, wild hay in the morning and to sit on the ground in the evening and watch the pale-faced emigrants climb in and out of the ox wagons and prepare their food. The women learned to sit without changing expression, weaving baskets or grinding food between the rocks while these strangers gawked as they walked around them. When these people spoke to them, they would simply stare, and if the talk continued the women would shake their heads or point to Cap John to show that he was in charge of the camp.

Thus did Cap John wax rich in worldly goods, in influence, and experience. His family, like his wealth, was constantly increasing. He was head of his own family, and the people who worked for him automatically looked upon him as a leader.

The white people who were settling in the Big Meadows respected Cap John and called him chief. So it came about that his following was as large as that of Big Chief Winnemucca. Because of this, a rift started among the Paiutes which grew wider and more serious as the years went by, and each Paiute took one side or the other. That is why history tells many things wrong about the settlement of this section of the country. You see, the historians got their information from the followers of Winnemucca or Natchez,[33] and not from the followers of Cap John.

6

SAU-TAU-NEE

SMILING at her reflection in the water, Sau-tau-nee carefully pushed her straight black hair into place. Then she applied the red paint to her cheeks, thinking how good it would be to be back at the karnee with her family again. She loved being bathed and clean once more. Living with a few women in the straggling outskirts of the village, eating no meat for three days and one more, and not seeing her family had given her a yen for action. How good it would be to run around camp seeing and talking to her older sisters and their little ones. To help her mother, to do any kind of work among her people, would be pleasant. To have the men around would be nice also. It had been lonely with only a few women. It was because of the men that she and the other women had to live on the outskirts of the camp for three or four days every month. These men, even the biggest and strongest, who were not afraid of wild, ferocious animals and could kill them with their bare hands, would turn pale at the thought of being near or of seeing the smallest woman in what the Indians termed the "time of flower." This was why on the outskirts of every village a few poor wikiups were left standing for the comfort of all women. At the end of the period each woman found a pool and bathed and applied the paint to her face as a sign that she was clean.[34]

For three years now, Sau-tau-nee had spent her allotted time each month at the edge of the camp, and the novelty of being a mature woman had worn off. Besides, there had been an air of excitement in the karnee when she came away. Purty-pour-no had come to visit from a near-by camp. She and her mother seemed wrapped in talk and every now and then they would look toward Sau-tau-nee as if they were talking about her. Purty-pour-no was looking for a woman for her young son, Scarface Charley.

In the Paiute country, when an Indian girl was old enough to marry, her mother, not the chief, was consulted. The boy's mother came to see the girl's mother and the two older heads made all the arrangements. Sometimes a boy would decide he desired a certain Paiute maiden and would persuade his mother to talk to her parent, but never, not under any circumstances, was the girl allowed to speak a word. She must be the wife of whoever was chosen for her. Sometimes she would put up a vicious fight, but in the end she was compelled to submit to the wishes of her parents, especially her mother.[35] This custom was so rigid it should have been called a law. In a few cases where the maiden had been defiant and had run away, all members of the tribe, even in distant villages, were obliged to catch her and return her to the home band to be stoned to death by members previously appointed for that duty. There was no divorce among the Paiutes.

No matter who was chosen to be the Paiute maiden's husband, no matter how untrue he was to her, or how many wives he took unto himself, regardless of how far away he roamed or where he lived with another woman, of how she loved and longed for another man, the once-married Paiute woman must remain true to her one and only husband as long as he was alive. The woman who under any circumstances was found untrue to her husband was stoned to death. This custom was not relaxed in any manner until after the white man came.[36]

Sau-tau-nee had no illusions about love and marriage. She knew Purty-pour-no had a tall, handsome son no older than herself with a scar across his face. But he was not the young man she wished her mother would pick for her. She knew she would have to be married some day. Every woman married in the course of time, but she hoped it would be many moons before a husband, no matter how handsome and brave, would come to claim her. [Despite her lack of enthusiasm, Sau-tau-nee and Scarface Charley were married, a fact not made clear in the text. Ed.]

Striking three black marks across her forehead and rubbing on some extra paint, putting on yellow dots to heighten her cheek bones, Sau-tau-nee rose from where she had been gazing at her reflection and tied a new grass woven skirt about her waist.[37] She had been practicing drawing with grease paint and had made live-looking yellow snakes up and down her legs.

During their enforced segregation, Sau-tau-nee and her companion had occupied their time making rouge and grease paint for the tribe. As they worked, they talked about the poor Shoshones who did not know the difference between cinnabar and limonite and had died from the poison. The Shoshones had broken open the beautiful red rocks from Cinnabar Mountain and rubbed it on their bodies. To bring out the color clearly, they moistened the rock with their tongues and later died. Those who did not paint themselves with this rock said their brothers had died because they had imitated the Paiutes.[38]

The Paiute Indians knew this was not true. They knew that this type of red rock was poisonous and was used only by their medicine man. Cap John's father knew how to extract the calomel. It was given in small dosages and he used it with his eagle feathers to cure the bilious and the very sick. Since the beginning of time the Indians have had rouge for their cheeks and grease paint for their skins. I still have mine. It was from a chunk given to me by a medicine man ten or twelve years ago. These cakes were distributed among the people so that everyone had his own, much as each white person has his own toothbrush.

The Indians did not have the cracked lips and chapped hands that they saw on the white men who came later into the country. They had a feeling of disgust for those men who had sores on their bodies which would never have been there had they used the cold cream like the Paiutes. The women saved deer tallow and elk bone marrow to make cold cream and grease paint. From a secret place the medicine man brought quantities of limonite and ochre. The girls boiled the material until the pure red or yellow sank to the bottom, and the trash and dirt came to the top to be skimmed off. It was then drained and poured into a mold. When it was firm, but not hard, it was mixed with the tallow and marrow until it was soft and creamy and soothing to the skin.

Sau-tau-nee felt so joyous and happy that she would have run all the way to camp had her arms not been loaded down with a big lump of grease paint which she had tried to wrap in tules. Everyone was so busy when she came swinging in with her load that they did not seem to notice how lovely she looked. Great piles of wee-pah, a certain kind of milkweed, were scattered on the ground and the women were sitting beside them making twine.[39] Sau-tau-nee knew without being told that they were getting ready for the annual mudhen hunt.

Making the cordage for the mudhen net was quite a responsibility. The net must be strong enough to hold hundreds of birds at one time. This was the first year Sau-tau-nee was allowed to make cord for the mudhen net. Only experienced women could make a cord 150 feet long with no knots and strong enough to be used in this net. This work kept the women of the tribe busy for a whole year. Each length of wee-pah twine was finished without a single knot and wound on smooth sticks and kept for the big net.

All the people came bringing wee-pah to help with the net. The young men who had been sent to hunt or fish brought fresh food for the women to cook. Those women working on the nets were relieved now and then. They would not stop to eat together but each took a handful when there was time. Even the men helped. They were stationed along the edge of the net to help keep the string taut and straight.

7

THE LAST GREAT PAIUTE COUNCIL

EVERY year when the chill of autumn was in the air and most of the mallards and teal had flown to a warmer climate, at the time when the mudhens came from other rivers and channels to live for the winter in the tule and willow coves of the Humboldt Lake, the chief of all the Paiutes summoned them to the annual council meeting.[40] At this time they caught and ate their favorite fowl, the mudhen. They also danced their prayers to the Big Man[41] and listened to the words of wisdom from the chief.

Instead of a dry alkali lake bed as the Humboldt Sink now is, at that time it was filled with water twelve feet deep in places and dotted with little islands. The Humboldt River then flowed into the northern end of Humboldt Lake. Carson Sink on the other end of the flat was also filled with water. Carson River, flowing north, emptied into Carson Lake. During high water time, the two lakes merged, giving the appearance of one big lake. That was why one of the history-writing pioneers first reported that the Carson River flowed south and was the outlet of a large lake. Returning later in the season when the water was low, he found that just the reverse was true. For many years, people who read about the winning of the West thought there was a river in the Great Basin that flowed north part of the year and flowed south the rest of the time. Winne-mucca and his band from Pyramid Lake, Old Truckee and the Indians from what is now Reno and Carson City, could come all the way by water, and some of them did; others took a shortcut across Ragged Top Mountain by Winnemucca Lake and Nightingale.[42]

After the entire tribe had assembled, it took a whole day to complete preparations for the hunt.[43] Tule flatboats were handled by those best on the oars and were sta-tioned miles out in the water to push and shoo the birds toward the mouth of the Humboldt.[44] The younger boys, women, and girls were placed at intervals in the bushes on land at the edge of the water. Cap John and Mo-be-ti-wak and the strongest men handled the big nets which were stretched across the mouth of the river. Everyone knew his position, everyone had to take part. Each person slept near his place so as not to frighten the birds by mov-ing in the early morning light.

Sau-tau-nee was placed at a vantage point not far from where the net was fastened. She was a little bit afraid. It was the first time she had slept so far away from her mother, father, or sisters. Now, she almost wished for Scarface Charley, but Cap John, whom she knew as a brother-in-law, was near by. Perhaps he would protect her from that monster of a man, Mo-be-ti-wak, who had a wing bone sticking from the septum of his nose. Until today she had never seen Mo-be-ti-wak, whose reputation for strength and wicked deception had been whispered through the entire tribe.[45] Sau-tau-nee ate a few tule roots, found a dry place, and lay down to sleep as she saw the other Indians doing. She slept well all night and awakened on a world with the sun coming over the mountains. She took her place and waited quietly as she had been told.

When the birds ventured out of the water, those stationed along the shore caught them and broke their legs instead of winging them. All the Indians knew the slim-legged skinny fowl could run faster than they could fly. Driving the mudhens into the net was careful and tedious business. A second net was stretched in back of the first, and as Cap John and Mo-be-ti-wak caught several hundred birds in its meshes, they pulled it out and gave it to the people waiting on land; these people killed the birds while the strong men took care of the next net.

After about three hours of shooing the birds toward the mouth of the river and into the net, the boats gradually came together in a semicircle. This gave some birds time to swim outside the boats and escape. Others dived between the boats and, swimming back of them, also escaped. Even so, the Indians had slaughtered thousands of them. When all the boats touched, the hunt was over. The men came ashore and everyone was busy for hours preparing for the feast to be held in the nearest village. This year, it happened to be Cap John's emigrant station where they cooked the mudhens. They fried some in grease, and jerked or dried others in the sun to keep for winter. They danced and chewed mudhen bones for three days.

Old Chief Winnemucca was in a good humor, but already he envied Cap John his emigrant station and his four wives. He longed for the beautiful American flag presented to Cap John by Frémont that was on display at the station. However, the year before, white travelers had presented Chief Winnemucca with a gift which had pleased him so much that he had called together the nearby bands of Paiutes to celebrate. He had since worn the gift as a regal headdress on all special occasions. This year, when he gave his words of wisdom to the two thousand people of the Paiute tribe, this priceless gift was tied grandly to his head. Old Chief Winnemucca's feeling of jealousy and outrage knew no bounds when he learned that the wonderful headpiece which he had worn with such pride was not to wear on his head but was a white dinner plate to be used to hold the food which he ate.[46]

After the Paiutes had returned to their homes from the fun and excitement of the mudhen hunt, the chief sent word that the white people had poisoned the water of the Humboldt River. Whole caravans of white families bound for California lay down beside the trail and died with no one left to bury them. This was the year of the great plague when cholera struck them down. Of the two thousand Paiutes, half or more died in the worst sickness that had ever come to the Indians. All the people were sick and many of them died. The fish lost their scales and died. The ducks lost their feathers and died. All the wild birds along the river died that year, too.

When the Paiutes first took sick, they screamed with pain. They rètched and purged and called for the medicine man and the witch doctor who tried all their cures—bleeding, the magic eagle feathers—to no avail, for soon they died. The people thought the white man had not only poisoned the river water but had bewitched the whole country. Desperately frightened, all the Paiutes, sick or well, started for the Pine Nut Range. When one was too sick to travel, he lay down and died. Some were dragged near a water hole and left alone, for the disease was so contagious that no one could care for the dead.

Scarface Charley was more afraid than most, and when

the others could not keep up, he left them behind. Sau-tau-nee's family had just made camp among the trees when her father was taken sick. All her life she remembered the few hours of his agony and how her mother tried to relieve him by putting hot ashes to his back as he lay beneath the trees. In spite of all she could do, the father died. They broke camp at once and left him unburied. As they started out again, brother Stephen took sick on the range just beyond White Cloud.[47] They left him to die and went to another spring. Only women were left, the mother and three daughters. On the way, they saw the dead and dying but did not stop to help them. Sau-tau-nee never forgot seeing one dead mother by the trail with a live child crawling over her.

The people who did not stop in the Pine Nut Range went on to Table Mountain. Pinenuts were plentiful and they gathered many for winter use. The custom was to make a holiday of gathering the pinenuts, but this season they made rich soup for those who had survived the disease. One day they heard someone holler. They looked toward the sound and saw smoke on the summit. When the voice came closer, they recognized Stephen. The tribe, what was left, began to scatter, scared to death of Stephen. He called to his mother, asking her not to run. One of Sau-tau-nee's sisters stopped to listen.

"I am not going to die," he said, "if I get food and water."

"I'm afraid of you. You're a dead man," the sister answered.

"I was sick, but I did not die," he said. "I could hear mother cry and I knew when you left me."

The mother, who had run with the others, turned and screamed at her daughter. "Stop talking to a ghost!"

"I'm not a ghost," called Stephen, "I'm your own son, Mother dear. Come closer and get some food and water for your starving child."

Because he talked so sensibly, the mother decided he was telling the truth. She called to the others and told them everything was all right. Stephen grew well and strong and was a great help to his family as he took his father's place. He lived to be a very old man.

The Indians determined not to return to the putrid water of the Humboldt. There was no disease among the pines, and the braves were afraid to venture away from them to hunt. The second winter, the pine nuts were so scarce you could count them on the trees. Many more died of starvation which they felt was the white man's fault, too. So when they returned to their old stomping ground, only about one-tenth of the original two thousand were alive.[48]

8

LIFE AND LEGENDS OF THE PAIUTES

I T was during the long stay in the mountains that Sau-tau-
nee had heard more stories about the white man. One
family had told of how, when they were living near the
Indian Caves,[49] only a mother, three girls, and a dog were
in camp. When the dog barked and they looked up and
saw a white man coming, they ran into the karnee. The
man called but the women didn't stir. The man came in
and made signs that he was hungry. The old woman gave
him a bowl of mush. The man put the bowl to his mouth
but the mush was cold and wouldn't run. He made motions about eating it. One of the girls giggled, crooked her
finger, and pretended to dip the mush from the bowl and
put it to her mouth. The man caught on and sat down and
ate the mush with his fingers and licked the bowl. Then
he stood up, pulled out his shirt-tail, took off his belt and
took out three gold-looking objects. He gave them to the
old one and went away. When their men came back from
hunting the woman told what had happened and asked
the men to put holes in the coins so that they could wear
them for ornaments. The metal was so hard they could
not bore holes in them. So, as they were no good, the Indians threw them away.

They told other legends during the long winter. They
had so little to do and so little was happening to take their

minds off their sorrows that they repeated these stories over and over, especially the ones told by those who had died.[50]

Sau-tau-nee's months of married life had been sad, but sorrow did not make her love or care more for this husband who had been chosen for her. She was such a little person that when she began to get fat the Paiutes laughed and told her she was as broad as she was long, and indeed, she did look as if she would burst at any time for the three months before Poodles was born. Just before she was confined, they boiled up lots of water. Every container that could be found was filled with water. The old women of the village gave her advice, but Scarface Charley, the cause of all this amazing roundness of her body, was not even in the village. They built a poor karnee and packed the boiled water over there. The medicine man had gone on a hunt, too. He was the doctor for all sicknesses, but he knew nothing about babies coming into the world nor did he want to know about such things. Men were afraid of women's blood.[51]

After she went to the karnee to have her baby, she could not see her husband or a single male relative for twenty-two days. If the men brought back deer or antelope, wild boar or mountain sheep, Sau-tau-nee could not have a bite. She could drink only the boiled water and eat ground-seed bread, pinenut soup, and vegetables for those twenty-two days. Pinenuts were very good and the tule leaves pulled from the ground were luscious, but there was so much pain to be endured. If she died, she would go to be with the Big Man who had left his footprints in the East Range.[52]

If she just suffered, she would have to bear the burden

she brought into the world on her back instead of in her stomach. Sau-tau-nee could not see much difference. In each case, the load was a burden that men had nothing to do with. Men had reason to be afraid of a woman at such a time. Once, a man had been caught out with his wife when it was borning time. He had helped and cared for her the best he could. The baby was fine and the mother lived to have other children, but the father's blood turned to water and he died from weakness before ten years had passed. Another man went near his wife before the twenty-two days were over and his blood clotted and turned to lumps so he could not go on the hunt.

As the years passed and hordes of caravans poured down the Humboldt Trail, the Indians lived more and more on what they could sneak from the white man. They understood more of what the whites said and could talk back with words like "God damn" and "fool." They had learned that the white men did not all have hair on their faces and that some of them had dark eyes.

The topography of the country was changing. The lakes in the sink were drying up and the Humboldt River no longer flowed into the lake but disappeared into the ground about twenty miles below Lovelock.

In those days the Paiutes stood together in everything.[53] With the main source of living gone, it was no more than natural for the Indians to drive off a few cows and horses left behind by the campers. Those animals were easy prey, but to get into camps and cut halters or unfasten the hobbles in spite of the guards was something else. It takes much doing to stalk a deer or outwit a fox, but hunting and bringing in the game had been what the Indian men were born for. Now they put all their tal-

31

ent and experience into outwitting the white man, thus taking home as much game as they had before, but of a different variety.

From the minute the Paiute first saw a man on a horse, his whole life was dedicated to owning and riding such an animal. It was as easy for a Paiute to ride a horse as for him to breathe. He did not have to learn how. He already knew. When it came to riding, the Paiute was a natural. So they took a horse and a cow now and then, which was not much considering that the whites had taken their antelope and deer. The Indians had to depend more and more on the beaver for food and warmth. The trappers coming down the Humboldt River had not only taken the beaver that were prime, but had gutted the streams that flowed into the river. After two trapping expeditions by the white men, the Paiutes knew that the beaver would never be plentiful in the Lovelock Valley again. So they banded together to cause the trappers as much trouble as they could, hoping to get them away from the river before all the beaver were gone.[54]

The Indians were told that soldiers had been stationed at Meachum's ranch to see that pilfering of food and horses was stopped. They couldn't catch the Indians who were stealing or doing anything that was wrong. They had to make good. So, they began to pay Indians to help them find other Indians who stole their horses. Old Chief Winnemucca and his cousin, Natchez,[55] were each given a horse because they had shown where the Indians had come to a spring near McDermitt. The soldiers killed all the Indians except for one girl who had run and hidden before they could kill her. This girl went about among the Paiutes of Lovelock Valley and told them how Winnemucca and Natchez had betrayed their own people. She said they were the only ones who knew where the spring was. With this information, the soldiers had waited in ambush to kill all of her family. When Chief Winnemucca rode his big bay horse and Natchez whizzed by on his white one, this girl encouraged the Paiutes to look the other way and to pretend not to see the gallant riders. So it came about that terrible hatred was borne in the souls of the people of Cap John against those of Winnemucca's and Natchez' band.[56]

Thus began the enmity within the Paiute tribe of Lovelock Valley which had been the cause of dissension and discontent for all of these years. Those Indians who believed the story of the betrayal of their people claimed Cap John for their leader, and the others stayed with Natchez when he became chief after old Winnemucca died.

9

JEROME LOWRY, THE SQUAW MAN

A FTER the battle of Pyramid Lake, Sau-tau-nee and the band of her tride came back to the Humboldt Lake and it was at about this time that they saw funny little brown men working with big oblong sticks and iron spikes, making a road with iron rails on each side.[57] The Indians were panic stricken when they saw these Chinese people, and they fled to Table Mountain. But food was so scarce that they had to come back, look to the white men, and beg. The white men would not let them come near their big tent, but the little brown men with the long pigtails of smooth, black hair gave them a new morsel to eat which they called rice. The Chinese fed the band of Paiutes who followed them all the way to Golconda.[58] Sau-tau-nee was with this band, traveling with Poodles on her back for weeks while the railroad was being built. At Golconda, the arch enemy of the Paiutes, the Shoshones, came down and pushed them out of the way. The Shoshones took the food left over for the Paiutes, and as they had nothing to eat, the Paiutes had to return to their old stomping ground.[59] When they reached old Oreana, the smelter was being built. Here they came, and the braves of the tribe brought wood for feeding the smelter.

The first intimation the Paiutes of Sau-tau-nee's band

had of the Oreana mill was when Scarface Charley brought some melted slag which he said was flowing like a stream of water and which the people called "malapai," meaning evil rock.[60] Sau-tau-nee's mother said that was a good name, for nothing good could come from rock that was melted and then turned out to be so hard even if the colors in it were beautiful. The rock was not allowed to come into the karnee. They were having enough bad luck anyway, what with all the white people coming into the valley and digging gold from the hills. There were several big tribes of white people who had made camp at places called Humboldt City, Unionville, and Star City. The people were going into the Unionville canyon and sleeping right between the mountains when everyone knew that no human being had slept in canyons since two grandfathers back, when the Paiutes had been in Cottonwood and Muddlebury canyons at the time when rocks fell down the mountain and the earth shook. The people held onto the sagebrush which came up from the roots. The earth trembled more than man had ever known.[61] Never after the big earthquake did the Paiutes sleep in a canyon, but these white tribes didn't heed the sign of nature sent by the Big Man.

They had plenty of food for themselves, though the animals that had been in the valleys had disappeared. The white men gave the red men food when they worked for them. There seemed to be no use fighting to keep the land where nothing grew any more. The seeds were nearly gone and it was necessary to be near the white people to get enough food on which to live. They did not want to be like the Shoshones and eat mice, snakes, bugs, and lizards. There were no fish in the streams as there had been before the white man came. Only at Pyramid Lake were the salmon and trout just as good as they ever were. They must keep that lake as their own reservation. The Paiutes were not warlike, but they had sent their best men to fight to keep Pyramid Lake.[62] Now the man named Wasson, who would give the shirt off his back to an Indian, was over there and would see that the great father at Washington did not take every piece of good land from the people who had always had it.[63]

Because Sau-tau-nee was so grounded in her beliefs of the Indian marriage customs, she was shocked when she learned that white men called young women into their dugouts or wooden houses and locked the doors. When a girl came out, she usually had some gift, maybe a piece of gold that could be traded at Cap John's store for blankets or head rags. Her mother had told her that the men who did the stoning had been killed when on the war path and that the women needed food which their men could no longer find when going on hunts. Scarface Charley had not come back for many moons. They heard he was making a marriage with a young woman down at Nixon. When he did come, he told them he had learned from the white people that he was not responsible for Sau-tau-nee and Poodles any more. Sau-tau-nee was sad, not because Scarface Charley had left her but because she was afraid she would be stoned to death if she were untrue to him.

She cut great bundles of sagebrush and chopped down trees for firewood to be used at the Montezuma Smelting Works.[64] The Indians were paid for this. The big monster that was built and that belched out so much black smoke must be worse than the animals of olden times which ate children and knocked down trees. Many times Sau-tau-nee had been told that they would get her if she did not behave, and this thing called the smelter put up by a Mr.

Nason was the biggest, most awful thing she could think of.[65]

Sau-tau-nee helped to gather the fuel, but she would not carry it to the smelter because she was shy and timid about seeing the white men who had built such a monster in the desert place near the river. The curse of the land was the alkali deposits stretching over it for miles, which contained lime and soda. It was used for flux, and the Indians were sometimes paid to scrape this up and bring it up to the office in buckets. The Paiutes still had a fear of these people, but the pangs of hunger caused them to forgive even the grossest insults.

By this time, Cap John was virtually chief of the band of Paiutes in the Lovelock Valley. He had a flair for making money and for making friends with the whites. His emigrant station at Carpenter's ranch had been quite successful, and now, since the mines were discovered in the Trinity Range, Humboldt City was thriving, and Star City had sent most of its population to Unionville. All the mines were sending their ore to the Montezuma Smelting Works at Oreana. Heretofore, they had sent it by ox team to the coast and the wagons stopped over night at Cap John's station. As there were fewer emigrants now and the ore wagons would pass by no more, Cap John moved his station to Old Oreana, a half mile from the present town on the Esspee.[66] Cap John had four wives and wanted Sau-tau-nee for his fifth. He wanted all his wives to sell themselves to the white men and bring the money to him. Two of these wives set uncomplaining to the task Cap John had set for them, but the others stubbornly refused.[67] Sau-tau-nee, although dependent on Cap John for food, refused to obey or to marry him. Scarface Charley was gone, Sau-tau-nee had no husband, and she had

Poodles to feed. The Indians agreed with Cap John that if she would not submit to him nor do his bidding in other ways, he had the right to beat her until she did. Two of his wives were Sau-tau-nee's sisters, who told her there was no use being stubborn, but Sau-tau-nee was still afraid that Scarface Charley might come back, and she was sure that if he did, the members of her tribe would stone her to death. So, despite her daily beating, she remained true to her husband.

One day, when Cap John was giving her an unmerciful beating and Sau-tau-nee was screaming at the top of her voice, a tall white man with blue eyes and reddish hair on his lip strode in and ordered Cap John to "Let that squaw alone."

"A big husky man beating a little woman like that is a shame," he said. "God damn you, stop it. Come on out here and tend to your business and sell me some fodder for these mules." Cap John minded the big white man, whose name was Jerome Lowry, and sold him an order of foodstuff besides.

When the big white man with the blue eyes and hair on his upper lip was ready to drive away, he said, "I need a wife. Get your kid, little woman, and come along with me." Sau-tau-nee, who was sitting on the ground, got up, took Poodles by the hand, and climbed into the wagon.

10

THE EARLY YEARS

FROM the day Lowry took them away in his wagon he called my mother "Susie" instead of by her beautiful Indian name, Sau-tau-nee (which means Willow Blossom), and Scarface Charley's child, Poodles, was called "Toodles" till the day she died.

Jerome Lowry and F. L. Carpenter were partners in the cattle business and were living in Oreana where the first precious metal smelter in the United States was going full blast. The partners had won a section of land in the Big Meadows, now known as the Lower Valley of Lovelock, in a gambling game with "Poker" Brown.[68]

For a time, Jerome and Susie lived at Oreana and every now and then Cap John came to ask Susie if she would come back to him. He still wanted her to be his wife. But Susie was true to Lowry from the day he kept Cap John from beating her. Very few men were ever loved as my mother loved Jerome Lowry. Her gratitude was pathetic. After they moved to Carpenter's ranch where I was born, Susie would see Cap John coming and run inside the dugout and shut the door. Cap John would come up and knock but she would not let him in. Then he would say, "It is your poor ole uncle, please let me in." But mother would make us stay quiet and still long after he was gone. On the other hand, if Lowry were there he would invite

Cap John in and talk to him. He would load Cap John down with sugar, salt, bacon, and flour to take away with him. Susie did not hold a grudge against her former suitor for the beatings he had given her, and after she got over her fear of him, they became good friends. After all, he was married to her sisters and, as the saying goes, "blood is thicker than water."

Cap John really was a fine man, tall and well built. From a certain custom of Paiute warriors, he had a hole punched in his nose to wear a wing bone through it. He sure was a good story teller and although he was blind, his voice was loud and clear. He used to call the young men out and lecture to them about how to live right. Sometimes he would call all the village out and tell them stories of how the animals acted when they were human. The people in Lovelock could hear him five blocks away and they used to ask the Indian boys what he was talking about. He lived to be nearly one hundred years old. I had already "taken the shawl"[69] and was living in the Indian village when Cap John died. I tried to get his family to go against custom and leave his flag and letter of recommendation from Captain Frémont for his people to keep, but they would not listen to me. They wrapped his body in the flag and put the paper beside him.[70] He was buried in the Indian graveyard which I had started when my little boy died. Several years after his death, one of Cap John's sons came and asked me about digging him up to get the flag and the paper.[71] This time I urged them not to desecrate his grave.

Lowry lived with Susie at Oreana for about a year, then he took her to the six hundred and forty acres in the Big Meadows to develop their ranching interest. The Carpenters stayed in Oreana to look after their holdings in that section of the country. On the ranch, Lowry built a dugout thirty feet long and fifteen feet wide. There was a good cookstove, a table, four chairs, a bedstead made of boards, and a straw-filled mattress, all in one room. Every few years as his family grew, Papa added to the dugout so we had plenty of room.

The problem of irrigation was the first to be solved. The Humboldt River was the source of water, but it was never dependable as some years it would be in flood, and other years, nearly dry. So the ranchers who were settling the country had many arguments and disputes over the division of the water. These disagreements were sometimes so serious they were carried to the United States Supreme Court in Washington, D.C. I remember one morning when we were having breakfast, Harry Fuss, who was batching on his ranch which joined Carpenter's and Lowry's, came in and without even saying good morning, said, "Lowry, what do you mean by cutting off my water?"

"What do you mean, 'cutting off your water'?" asked Lowry.

"Well, the water does not flow from the slough into the ditch. You have certainly cut it off."

Mike McGovern, who was working for Jerome then, said, "Fuss, we finished irrigating three days ago. We have not been using your water."

"Come on," Lowry said, "we will see what happened to the water." When the men went out, Mother told us to follow behind and watch what happened. She was afraid because Fuss had a shovel. When we had walked about a mile from the house, we came to a narrow place in the slough, about sixteen feet wide. There was the prettiest beaver dam you ever saw! Each willow stick was cut on a slant; at the bottom, where it was wide, one willow branch was laid one way and one the other, just as even as if it had been figured out by a human being. Tules and grass were filled in so that the water could not go through. It was absolutely perfect. The men opened the dam enough for the water to flow into the Fuss ditch. Discovering that the beavers had been the cause of Fuss not getting his water, the men laughed and walked back to their ranches in high good humor.[72]

My father was a big, fine-featured, handsome man. He was over six feet tall with light sandy, curly hair. He used to bring men to the dugout to visit. Carpenter came often, both before and after they moved to the ranch from Oreana. Pete Anker, another homesteader, came, and also newcomers who were looking over the Big Meadows for a location. Mark Twain used to come, but all I remember about him was his whiskers and that he rode an old white plug of a horse. Jerome had his picture which was autographed.[73]

Lowry never liked to see a woman imposed upon. One day, when he was riding the range, along came an Indian on a nice pony. Behind him trudged his woman with a papoose on her back and laden with a pack of groceries. Papa made the Indian get off his horse, pack the groceries, and walk, while the woman with the papoose rode the horse. He followed them a long way, for he knew the Indian would get on his horse as soon as Papa was out of sight.

11

MY EDUCATION

IN the vague hope that I would grow into an intelligent,
attractive "Indian Princess" whom he could parade before his hated stepmother back in Virginia,[74] my father
took me from our dugout home to begin my education in
a one-teacher school.

My father named me "Annie" for his sister and with pa-
tience saw to it that I spoke my first words in English
rather than the Indian tongue. He had run away from
home when he was thirteen or fourteen, and while he was
clever, well-read, and a wonderful businessman, he did
not reckon with the forces of Indian training and tradition. His vain, silly ambition would have had more chance
of coming true if his work had kept him home after I was
four or five years old. Then he could have attended to my
education. Instead, when he was at Blue Wing[75] on the
cattle range and at Lowry Wells,[76] which he dug from a
spring, he would be gone for six weeks at a time. However, when he was home, he insisted that I speak good
English and discouraged all Paiute talk.

During the time that my father was away, Toodles and
Mother, my little brother, Robert, and I would see no one
but Mike McGovern, the hired man. Then we would re-
vert to Indian life. Toodles and I would race over the
plowed fields and play in and out of the sage and rabbit

45

brush. Sometimes Mother would put brother Robert on her back and we would go out and hunt wild berries and seeds. We ate the wild berries and learned to grind the seed between the rocks to make Indian meal that tasted real good.

During those days she told us stories of Indian lore and legends of old customs that had, for generations, been handed down by word of mouth in the Paiute tribe. Besides this, she explained what the white man's coming had done to the country along the Humboldt Trail and how it had affected the Paiute Indians. We took long tramps, going as far as the Lovelock Cave. Long before it was "discovered" we learned how our ancestors, the Nu-mahs, destroyed the Sa-duc-ca tribe by suffocating them with smoke in the Lovelock Cave.[77]

One of the rare days when my father was home, he said, "Annie, would you like to live with Mrs. Carpenter for awhile?" I nodded my head.

"Don't shake your head like a Paiute Indian," he scolded. "Say, 'Yes, Papa,' or 'No, Papa.' "

"Yes, Papa," I repeated.

"That's good," he said. Then as if to himself, he added, "Pa couldn't make me say 'Yes, sir,' or 'No, sir,' so I'll not try it on Annie."

The next day, Mr. Carpenter came and I went with him to Oreana. It was my first experience living in a house. In our dugout home on the ranch we cooked, ate, and slept in the same room. It was pleasant living at the Carpenters'. I liked their three boys. Willie was about my age, maybe a bit younger. There was Lumie, named for his father, Luman, and Charlie, just a little fellow learning to walk.[78] We fished in the crooked part of the Humboldt River and played games like tag and hide-and-seek.

Not long after old man Carpenter brought me back from Oreana, Papa, without talking to me, arranged with Mrs. Emmons in Lovelock for me to board with her and go to school. Papa gave Mrs. Emmons orders that I was not to go home until he came for me; that I was to have nothing to do with the Indians, not even to speak to my cousins or my aunts. He tried to take me to spend the afternoon with my mother and brothers every third Sunday when he was out on the cattle range at Blue Wing and Lowry Wells. However, it would sometimes be three months before I could go home. Any time during those long months, I was so homesick I could have died.

Papa gave instructions to Mrs. Emmons about caring for me. She was to teach me how to make my bed and take care of my room but she could give me no other work. She was to comb my hair every morning and see to it, when I started to school, that I was clean and as well-dressed as any white child. I was to wear white starched aprons. These had pockets trimmed in red and were tied in a bow at the back.

The first schoolhouse in Lovelock was a one-room building painted grey with two entrances, one for the boys and one for the girls. The boys played on one side of the grounds and the girls on the other. Inside, the walls of the room were painted a dingy white or grey with varnished oak wainscoting. Mrs. Holt was my first teacher. I was the first Indian in Lovelock to go to school with white children. Perhaps I was the first person of the Paiute tribe to go to school at all.[79]

My schoolwork was easy and for a long time I was treated like any other pupil and did not realize that the white people looked down on me or that there was a difference between me and the white children. I was considered one of the older girls, and while I was friendly with girls of my age, at recess time I loved to play with the little girls because I wanted an excuse to exercise.

One crisp October morning the air was so exhilarating that no young person, certainly not an active Indian girl, wanted to be inside a house. Dressed in my white apron that Mrs. Emmons kept fresh for me, I was on my way to school when I met Cora Williams. She was all excited.

"They buried Ching Lee last night," she whispered, "and our Chink cook said they put enough food on his grave to last three days until he gets to glory."

"Who is going to eat it?" I asked.

"They think his spirit will need the food," she said. I knew from her expression that Cora had something in mind but I waited until she said, "Let's play hooky and go to the graveyard."

"Hooky?" I asked. "You mean not go to school this morning?"

Cora nodded. "Ching Lee said when the last Chinaman died, the food was all gone in three days. If we get over there before the Indians, we'll get a good feed and the Chinese will think the spirits ate it."

The idea of something to eat or fooling the Chinese appealed to me less than the longing I had to spend the morning out of doors.

Our school was the last building on the edge of town, and the cemetery was just across the slough. While we were trying to get across this muddy water we heard Cora's small sister, Maude, screaming, "Wait for me, Cora, wait for me."

"You go back. You are too little," said Cora. "Go to school like a good girl."

"I want to go with you," she said.

"No. You're too little. The Chinese ghost might get you," Cora answered.

"If you don't let me go, I'll go back and tell Mama you are playing with Annie," said Maude.

The significance of Maude's last words, "playing with Annie," was lost on me.

"Alright," hastily answered Cora. "If you keep your mouth shut you can come. But if you talk or cry, we will tell the Chinese ghosts to get up from their graves and eat you."

Somehow we got Maude across the slough and hid in the sagebrush until we heard the school bell ring. Then we moved to where there were a few graves. We found a bare spot surrounded with rabbit brush. Here we told Maude to sit and watch the food as we brought it from the grave.

I placed my books on a rock and carefully folded my white apron over them. Watching for miners or Indians, and always keeping out of sight when any figures appeared, we slipped to the grave and returned with bowls of chicken and rice and a few pieces of ginger candy. Instead of the usual brown Chinese jar of rum, there was a goblet of whiseky. Crouching and trying not to show her head above the sagebrush, Cora was carefully holding this goblet when we heard a voice.

"Oh yes, I'm going to tell that you are playing hooky." It was Frank Mulvaney, the Irish boy whose greatest joy was teasing the girls.

"You are playing hooky yourself," said Cora.

"Like fun I am. The teacher sent me to find you." Instinctively I knew that this was not true.

"Frank, that is not so," I said. I thought Frank might be trying to get out of school that day, too.

"If you will give me plenty to eat and drink," he said, "I won't tell on you."

"You can have this liquor," Cora told him, "if you promise never to tell." Frank agreed, and taking the glass from Cora, he gulped down three or four big swallows.

"Good golly, that's strong. You'd better have some," he said, and handing the glass to Cora, he sat down. Cora took a sip and passed it on to Maude and me. Frank started to rise but something had happened to him. He staggered and fell. We thought it very funny so we got up and pretended to be drunk, too, and would laugh and fall down and laugh some more.

We were having such a good time eating the food and taking our sips, and falling down and laughing hard that we did not realize so much time had gone by—when behold, the school dinner bell rang! With no thought of secrecy now, we put the bowls back on poor Ching's grave. I grabbed my books, put on my white apron, and ran home as fast as I could.[80]

One Sunday after I had been in school several months, Susie Lumkin, a relative who worked for Mrs. Emmons, was combing my hair and said, "Annie, did you know that your Papa was going to put your Ma out and take you away from her?" I did not answer because I thought this could not be true. But the next day after school when I was changing my apron up in my room, I heard voices below. Listening, I recognized Mrs. St. Clair's voice. Remembering her black, shiny hair and how Papa used to make over her, I lay down on the floor, put my ear to a crack and heard her say, "Yes, Lowry, I would take those children and put them where people would never know they were Indians." She went on, "You're a nice looking man, Jerome Lowry. I wouldn't live with that old squaw."[81]

"Yes, you're right, I'll go." I heard my father's voice. "As soon as the boys are old enough, I'll put Annie in a convent and take them with me. I've already bought a place in Oregon."

It was hard to believe that my father was talking about leaving my poor mother. I got off the floor and went down into the back yard. Feeling lonely and distressed, I was looking through a crack in the back yard fence when I saw my mother. She carried a pack of groceries on her back and a little boy, my brother Jack, on her shoulder. I stood a box on top of a keg of nails, climbed up, jumped over the fence, and followed her. When I was about two hundred feet behind, Jack turned and saw me.[82] Of course he kept looking back at me.

"Be still, Jack," Mother told him. "You are heavy when you wiggle so." But Jack kept turning to look at me.

"What are you looking at?" she asked Jack. Then she turned and saw me behind her.

"Daughter, dear," she said to me, "what are you doing here?" I tried to tell her what I had heard.

"Maybe he was just talking," she said. She turned to go and I walked along with her.

"Did you get permission to come?" she asked.

"No," I answered.

"How did you come?"

"I ran away," I told her.

"You had better go back." She began walking faster but I followed for a little while. She said a second time, "You'd better go back. When your Papa comes, he will whip you real hard."

"No," I said, "I'm going with you."

Mother started toward home without saying more. I was happy, so happy, to be home. The next day when I saw a wagon coming, I ran to the field. It was Mr. Emmons and his son. After the wagon left, I returned to the dugout. "Old man Emmons came after you," Mike McGovern said. "Next time he come, you not here, he will get in and lick you good."

Nothing he said could scare me. I was at home. I was on top of the world. For three weeks, my brothers and I would run away every time we saw a wagon coming. Then Jerome came home. When he found out about me he was raging mad. The way he talked to my mother was a shame. It was not her fault I had run away. She did not know enough English to talk back to him. She tried to keep me from following her that first day, and every day since then she had told me I ought not to have run away. After he had vented his spleen on Susie, he called me. "Why did you leave Emmons'?" he asked.

"I saw Mama and brother Jack," I said. "I just jumped over the fence and followed them."

He gave me a good whipping with a willow switch, got me cleaned up, and took me back to Mrs. Emmons' in Lovelock. Back in school, I was faced with the fact that running away was useless. My teachers, Mrs. Holt and Miss McIntyre, who later became Mrs. Harry Wingate, both helped me to settle into the routine of school life.

Of several comical incidents which stand out in my memory of school, there was one of seeing Francis Reid, youngest of the Reid family,[83] wearing a sunbonnet when he went to school. He was such a little shaver that he looked like a grasshopper walking. I liked him and all the Reid boys. They were kind and understanding. They treated me as an equal and never tried to take advantage of me because I was an Indian.

Another time, I showed Maude Williams how the Indians extracted rubber from rabbit brush and we used it for gum.[84] She and I often slipped away from school to get it. When Miss McIntyre caught us chewing it in school, she took it away from us. Once when we had a good supply, she asked us for it. We told her we had none. Then Cora, who was peeved at Maude for not giving her any, told the teacher we had wads of gum stuck under our desks. In front of the class, Miss McIntyre gave us a good scolding which made us ashamed for fibbing. But we were more disgusted with Cora for being a tattle-tale.

Mrs. Emmons and Susie Lumkin must have tired of combing my long brown hair because one day after I had lived with them for about three years, they cut my braids, leaving my hair short. When Papa came a few weeks later, the first thing he did was to notice my heavy braids were gone. He was so raging mad that he took me from Mrs. Emmons' and had me board with the George Singers. They lived in an adobe house which had three rooms upstairs. Singer had come from Germany and later sent for his wife and little son, Enos.[85] I enjoyed helping Mrs. Singer with the English language while I lived with them for a year and a half. After that, I lived at home. My brothers and I had our own horses and rode to school. When our ranch neighbor's daughter, Etta Theis, was old enough to go to school, she sat behind me on my horse.

By this time, Lovelock's school had outgrown the one room. Pete Anker, a first rate carpenter, had built a little two-story schoolhouse with a cupola which housed the bell. I spent my last school days there. A few years later, when they built the high school, this building was moved and became a town residence.

At school, my favorite subjects were arithmetic and spelling. I was good in both, and in spelling I was usually at the head of the class. Every Friday afternoon we had a special program. About once a month we had a spelling bee. To arrange for this the teacher named two pupils—a leader from each side. After these two drew straws to see who would choose first, they chose alternately until all the class was on one side or the other. Then, from McGuffey's blue-back speller, the teacher gave out words to spell—first to one side then the other. Any person missing a word had to sit down. The teacher continued to give out words until all but one on one side was spelled down. The side who had the last speller standing, won. I enjoyed this game very much and looked forward to the Friday which had spelling-bee time.

One day we chose sides and spelled for a prize. All the spellers had been spelled down except Emmett Reid on one side and me on the other.

"Emmett," said the teacher, "spell 'nozzle.' "

Emmett: "N-o-s-h-i-l."

"Annie, spell 'nozzle.' "

Annie: "N-o-z-z-l-e."

I received a gold pin and was so proud and happy, but Cora's mother was awful mad. She raised Cain. She said to Cora, "I wouldn't let that little Paiute spell me down." Then Mrs. Williams came to school and before everybody she said, "I know that little Paiute is not smarter than my girl. She ought not to be in school anyway." And to the teacher, Miss Emma Cutting, she said, "Why don't they put her out?"

When Lowry heard this, he came to school and talked

to the teacher. He hunted up Mrs. Williams and said, "Don't you ever speak again about putting my child out of school. I am one of the biggest taxpayers in the district and I'd better never hear of such a thing again."

On other Fridays, we were given verses to memorize and recite. Papa helped us at home with these. He taught us how to bow when we came on the rostrum to speak. He showed us how to use gestures to make the words more emphatic. He used to say, "Don't say your lines in a singsong like those ignorant whites." Then he would singsong "Ta-ta-ta-ta-ta-ta-ta-ta-ta." I had to learn the "American Flag." He rose like an orator and said, "Stand up straight, open your mouth, and speak out."

"When freedom from her mountain height,
Unfurled her standard to the air;
She tore the azure robe of night
And set the star of Glory there."

He taught brother Robert to recite "The Boy Stood on the Burning Deck." That was too long for a little boy but Robert learned it, every word with all the gestures, and got up and said the piece in school. Papa used to say, "Be proud of your country and your flag. When you go to speak, stand up, open your mouth. Don't slouch and act ashamed like poor white trash."

My last year at school was interesting and exciting. Miss Mary Wilson, now Mrs. Steve Young, was my teacher. I loved to ride horseback and could outride any of the boys or girls of Lovelock. But one day, I was racing with my brothers and my horse stumbled and fell, and I broke my arm. I could not ride to school while my arm was in a sling so Papa had me board with Mrs. Emmons for six weeks while the break healed.

Thus it was again that I found myself in my old room,

my ear to the floor, listening to my father tell the women downstairs that he had sold his ranching interests here and was moving his stock to his acreage in Oregon. He began to tell his plans for me. He had made all arrangements for me, not only to enter the convent but to keep me there until I graduated. Then he would come and take me to his home in Virgina, and from there I was to enter an Eastern women's college. I didn't know where and I didn't care. I could only think, "He's breaking up our home. He is leaving my poor broken-hearted mother to shift for herself, and I won't go with him. He can't make me go." Later, he pleaded with me, he cajoled, even threatened my very existence, but I would not go with him. After my father left Lovelock Valley, I never went to school again.

12

SHIFTING FOR OURSELVES

IT took my father several weeks to wind up his business, make his wagons ready, and round up fourteen hundred head of cattle. They say this was the first time such a large herd raised in the Big Meadows had been taken out of Humboldt County on a cattle drive. Everyone who could, came to the edge of town to see the big drive get under way. Jerome Lowry was a big man in the county and everyone liked him. His crew was made up of cattlemen and cowboys and Indians from around Lovelock. Scarface Charley was one who went with my father to the end of the drive.[86] My father never told me anything about his business. Actually, what I have just related was really only just hearsay.

For two or three years before this, my father had been taking my brothers, Robert and Jack, with him when he was out on the range in the summer. I know now that he was weaning them away from our mother, so when he was ready to leave her for good, they went with him as a matter of course. While he was making his preparations he came to the dugout with the boys a few times. They played around, visiting with mother, while Jerome spent his time trying to persuade me to go with him to his new home.

When my father realized that I was determined not to

leave my mother, he promised me after he got settled he would come back for Susie and me. Later, while we were waiting for his return at the dugout, Scarface Charley came back and told the Indians that my father had married a white woman in Idaho. When this information reached us, I knew that he had no intention of living with my mother again. After a few more weeks had passed, we heard that he was on his way back. Fearing that he would force me to leave my mother and return with him, we ran away and hid. The country at Big Meadows is level and covered with sage and rabbit brush, so anyone walking there could be seen for miles. To keep him from finding us, we stayed under cover of brush in the daytime and came out after nightfall to rummage for food which was so scarce we nearly starved. When we found out that Lowry had given up looking for me, and had left Lovelock for good, we returned to our dugout home on the ranch.

We were only there a couple of days when Frank Carpenter told us that he had bought Jerome Lowry's half of the ranch, which included the dugout shelter, and that he needed it to house the men who worked for him. Sadly, we moved from our home to the Indian Colony in Lovelock where we lived in an abandoned karnee and ate what the rest of the Indians could give us, which was not much. My mother was very miserable. She used to cry for hours and was so distraught she would roll on the floor and moan. This made me feel my father's harshness more than anything else.

One day, a woman and a little boy about four years old came to visit us. The little boy asked mother for some bread to eat and Mother told him she had none. The little boy got mad and said he was going to burn the house down because we had no bread. While we were playing the rag and stick game,[87] not paying any attention to the boy, we found that our grass karnee was on fire. It blazed so suddenly that we could not save any of our belongings. It was at this time that we lost my father's Bible which contained all his records of our births and a few mementos which we prized.[88]

Shortly after the karnee burned, Carpenter came and told me that Lowry had left me in his keeping and that I must go home with him. When I refused to go he left, saying that he would send the sheriff after me. I knew he was telling the truth, so Mother and I ran away. Following the Humboldt River, we foraged for berries and roots that grew along the way and finally reached Winnemucca where my mother's sister and family lived.

Jenny Harris, who was my cousin and Cap John's daughter, had a job waiting table at the Lafayette Hotel. One Saturday afternoon when Jenny and I were going down town, a lady called to us. It was Mrs. Ed Kelly, wife of the editor of the local newspaper, the *Silver State*.[89] She said to Jenny, "Who is this girl?"

Jenny said, "She is my sister." Indians could not distinguish between their cousins and sisters.[90]

"Where is she from?" she asked.

"Lovelock," Jenny told her.

"What is her name?" she asked.

"Her name is Annie Lowry."

"Annie," Mrs. Kelly turned to me, "do you want to work for me?"

"Yes," I answered. I did not know about work, but I said "Yes."

"You take care of the kitchen, keep it clean, wash the dish towels, clear the table, wash the dishes, and sweep

the kitchen. You will be free for the afternoon for two bits
a day."

I started to work the following morning. On the next
Sunday morning, I was paid. I got one dollar and a half
for one week. There was so much money, I couldn't count
it. It looked so big, I didn't know where to put it. Anyway, I did not spend it. I worried and wondered what to
do; then I buried it under the stump of a tree. Every little
while I would run out to see if it was still there. I used to
take the money out and lie on my belly under the nearby
tree. I would lay the two-bit pieces edge to edge on the
palm of my hand, and by turning my fingers a little, I
could balance them across my palm. But I was not
satisfied, so I tied the money in a rag and put it in my
stocking where it made a big bulge at my ankle.

The next day when Jenny was going to buy a new dress
at Rhinehart's Store, I decided to spend some of my
money and buy a new dress, too. I watched Jenny as she
selected an awfully pretty piece, indigo with white
flowers on it, and a bunch of tape to trim it in. Calico was
eight and a half cents a yard and I could get six yards and
trimming for four bits. When she was through buying,
Jenny said, "Now you buy."

I had a piece already spotted. Mine was indigo, too, but
with a white diamond check. I also bought the tape. Then
Jenny said, "You buy a spool of thread." I did. After we
got out of the store, Jenny told me to unwrap the package
and we would put the two pieces of goods together with
the thread. She said we would go to Mrs. Bonifield's, who
would make a dress for two bits and a dime.[91] Jenny
asked Mrs. Bonifield to sew for her. She said she wanted
her to make a dress.

"How do you want it made?" she asked.

"A gathered skirt, waist with a square yoke, and tape," said Jenny, "and long sleeves with tape, and three rows of tape around the skirt."

"Have you the thread?" the lady asked.

"Yes," said Jenny.

"I bought that thread," I said.

"Shut up," said Jenny. "You do not know what you are talking about."

"You are not going to have it," I yelled. I grabbed my cloth with the thread and went alone to Mrs. Kelly's. This was in the afternoon and Mrs. Kelly was cooking and as my work was done, I went to my favorite tree and lay on my belly and watched for Jenny to come to the hotel to work. I felt blue to think Jenny was going to get her dress made before I was.

By the end of the next week, I had very little left of the first week's wages. This time Mrs. Kelly sent me down to the printing office to collect my pay. When I went in, Mr. Kelly looked up from his desk and said, "Well, here's my girl, what do you want?"

"Mrs. Kelly sent me here for my pay," I answered.

Mr. Kelly got up from his desk, pulled out a drawer, took out the money and handed it to me. I took the money he gave me, but did not look at it until I got back to the house, went in and asked Mrs. Kelly if she needed me. "No," she said, "not for an hour yet." I went out and lay down under my tree to count. Mr. Kelly had given me one dollar and seventy-five cents in two-bit pieces!

"By George," I said, "he gave me too much." I laid the quarters on my hand. I never saw such a long string of money. When I looked up, I saw Jenny going to work in her new dress. I couldn't stand it any longer. I got up and walked straight to Mrs. Bonifield's house.

"Hello," I said. "Won't you please make my dress?"

"How do you want it made?" she asked.

"Just like Jenny's."

"All right," she answered, "I'll make it up for you." While she was measuring me, she looked up and said, "Jenny got mad."

"Yes," I told her. "But it was my thread." I had enough money to pay for making the dress and to buy a pair of shoes at Rhinehart's. The shoes cost a dollar and twenty-five cents and Mr. Rhinehart threw in a pair of stockings. I was all rigged out.

Mrs. Kelly, Mrs. Germain, Mrs. Torrilton, and Mrs. Rhodes were all related. They were great for giving family dinners. I went from one place to another as dishwasher. One day, all dressed up with the shoes that hurt a little, I went to the hotel where my cousins were working. When I came in, the older cousin said, "How nice you look, Annie. I'm glad you have a place to work." But Jenny just looked me up and down and said nothing. She would never tell me I looked nice or give me a compliment and always seemed to be jealous of me.

Mrs. Kelly was a fine woman. She was kind and helpful and taught me many things. I stayed with her a little over a year until, one day while I was at work, an Indian came and told me that Jerome Lowry had been in Lovelock looking for me and had just arrived in Winnemucca to take me away with him. With not a word to Mrs. Kelly, I ran to my mother and told her what I had heard. Without saying goodbye to anyone or even taking our few belongings, once again Mother and I ran away and hid. We lived for days on the scarcest amount of food, only a few potatoes that we could find in the fields left behind by the harvesters. We finally got back to Lovelock, starved and thin. We were sorry sights. Our shoes were about worn out and our clothes not much more than rags. We lived with Toodles, my half-sister, Scarface Charley's daughter who had married a man named Sanny and had a little girl about two years old.

One day several Indians were sitting in front of Young's store and I was leaning against a post, when I heard a knock on the window. Turning, I saw Steve Young motion me to come over. I was too scared to move. He knocked again and the other Indians told me to go but my heart was pounding so hard, I simply could not move. Then he came to the door and called, "Annie, come over. I want to see you." One of the girls offered to go with me, so I crept inside the store. Mr. Young asked me what I had to eat and I told him "just what we could work for."

He looked at the rags I wore for stockings and the holes in my shoes. "Pick out a pair of shoes and some clothes," he said. "Your father is going to pay for this. He is your father and I will see that he pays for what you need in food and clothes."

My heart was beating so hard that I couldn't talk. The girl with me asked him to give me a pair of stockings so I could try on the shoes. Mr. Young gave me the stockings and told me to put them on while he went to the front of the store. Besides the shoes and stockings, he gave me material for dresses for mother and me.

Susie got work in the fields and I took care of Toodles and her little girl. One day, I came in to find Toodles lying on the floor, heaving violently. I knew that she was pregnant and had had no food for several days. As my sister lay there moaning, I thought, "I can't let her starve to death." Without a word, I left the karnee and went straight to Steve Young. I told him what the conditions were. He gave me a load of groceries which I took on my back.

When I emptied the bag on the floor in the karnee, there was flour, beans, salt pork, and baking powder. I cleaned up the floor and then mixed bread. I put it on a baker–frying pan[92] on the live coals on the hearth in the center of the karnee. Toodles sat up and ate a little. From that day, she ate what she wanted and for a while seemed to improve, but she was never well again. Toodles died before her second baby was born. She left her husband Sanny, and a little girl, Julia.[93]

We burned the karnee where Toodles died. Sanny went back to his mother's to live. Mother and I took Julia to raise, and the three of us lived with relatives until we could build a karnee of our own.

13

ANNIE DOUGHNUTS

I T was an ancient custom of the Paiute Indians to burn the karnee where one of their tribe had died. They believed that otherwise the spirit of the departed would return. In later years, when the government took over, we were made to understand that we were not to burn these houses as we did our karnees; when anyone died after that, to simulate our usual custom, we boarded up the entrance and opened up a new doorway. We also turned the house around on the lot or moved it to a different location.[94]

With the help of the other Paiutes, we gathered the willow boughs and tules. First, we made a number of tule mats. These were two-and-a-half by eight feet. A frame made of willows was woven in and out with layers of tule leaves. The uprights of the house were made of large willows planted in a circle about two-and-a-half feet apart. These willows were about ten feet long. Beginning about four feet from the ground, they were drawn gradually toward the center to make a slanting roof. They were not brought completely together, for a hole had to be left for the smoke to go through the top. The Paiutes made the best and strongest twine, thread, and rope from the bark of a bush which was something like a milkweed. Then they tied the mats securely to the willows and had a karnee both rain and wind proof. Nearly always, they built a windbreak of willows and brush just outside the karnee which they used as the white man does his front porch.[95]

When the murder of Annie Doughnuts occurred, Mother and I were living in a tule house near Bungey Jim and his family. So we all knew about what took place and I saw the whole thing with my own eyes. But I, who could have simplified the case at every trial by telling what I knew, was never asked to testify. It was probably a good thing for me that I was not called before the court in that capacity, for if I had told only what I had seen, I might not have lived to be here now and tell what happened.

Sometimes I wonder at the white people who are so smart and think they know so much. They do things as dumb as Indians in spite of all their high-falutin' talk. In this case, it might not have been as much dumbness as fear, though I did not realize it then. Johnny Reid, the scientific white man who had cultivated the friendship of the Paiute Indians for years, said when the trials were over that the white men were afraid to hang Bungey Jim.[96] So maybe they did not want to make too strong a case against him. The Paiutes were naturally friendly to the whites, but the white people were not sure, and as they did not understand Indian ways, they did not trust Indian motives.

Annie Doughnuts was a big, fat Shoshone Indian from the Reese River country who had taken up with a white man named John Tee. When they came to Lovelock they brought with them a little half-breed girl, the child of her dead sister. The man was a prospector and Annie Doughnuts went with him everywhere, doing his cooking and tending camp. When they made Lovelock their headquarters, the woman talked with the Paiutes and told them she

was a witch. There was some talk of her having bewitched a child who died, but as the Shoshone and Paiute
tribes were not friendly we did not get definite information along that line. Finally the white man died near Pyramid Lake and Annie Doughnuts came back to Lovelock
to live in the Paiute Indian Colony. She worked for white
people and made a good living for herself and the little
girl, and in about two years, Carson Charlie took her for
his wife.

At that time the Southern Pacific depot had a platform
around it and the Indians used to sit on the platform and
gamble. One day Bungey Jim's woman and Annie Doughnuts were playing a game when they got into a dispute
over a gambling debt.

"I win, I win the bet," said Bungey Jim's woman.

"No, it's mine," said Carson Charlie's woman, and she
grabbed the money.

"Take it," cried Bungey Jim's woman. "I hope you buy
something to eat with it, and you eat it and die."

"What about you?" returned the witch woman. "You
are not going to live long yourself."

Two or three months went by and Bungey Jim's woman
took sick. She drank water and took some herbs but did
not get well. They sent over to the Indian Reservation at
Nixon for an Indian doctor.[97] He came and worked all the
signs over her but she did not improve. He used his eagle
feathers and went into a trance but nothing he did helped
the sick woman. Finally, he gave up.

"A witch woman has her in her power," he told them. "I
cannot do anything." Bungey Jim got all his family together, his father, his mother, and his sisters, and they
talked over what they should do. They decided to ask
Carson Charlie's woman to come and take away the evil

spell. If she did not take it away, they would kill her so the evil would go with her.[98]

It was Bungey Jim who went to see Annie Doughnuts. He talked to her and asked her to come and take away the spell from his wife so she would get well again.

"No," said the woman. "I have nothing to do with her sickness. She got sick on her own."

"If you don't come up to the karnee and make my woman well," Bungey Jim said, "we are going to kill you. You come tomorrow."

"I'll be up a little after dinner," promised the woman. "I have to work in the morning."

The next morning while working for Mrs. Hill, Annie Doughnuts told her about Bungey Jim's visit.

"Maybe some morning, I no come." she told Mrs. Hill. "You know then I be dead."

After our work on the following day, while we were resting and talking, Mother and I saw Annie Doughnuts coming on the trail between our two karnees.

"There she comes, Annie," said my mother. "She is a fool to go up there."

All the women were gathered at Bungey Jim's. Annie Dougnuts passed us and went into his karnee.

"I'm hungry," said Sam, who was with us at the time.[99]

"Get wood for a fire, Annie," said my mother, "and start to cook something."

I went over to the rabbit brush growing between the two karnees and was stooping to get an armload when I heard a scream.

"Don't, don't! Please don't do that!" cried Annie Dough-nuts. She was kneeling at the bedside of Bungey Jim's wife. His sister was standing over her with a hatchet in her hand. She began beating Annie Doughnuts. She hit fast, blow after blow, until Annie Doughnuts fell almost out of the doorway.

"They've killed the witch woman," I screamed, running to our karnee.

Sam, Mother, and I watched every move. The women were milling around. Bungey Jim took the hatchet.

"Cut her face up," said the woman. "Cut it up good."

"She will come back if you don't kill her good," said one sister. Bungey Jim came out and with one swift lick, he cleft one side of her face from eye to ear. It was terrible to see, but we did not want to miss any of it. Mother said she was going over. We urged her not to go but she insisted and was nearly over there when Bungey Jim came out.

"Go back, you go back," he called to her. "We don't want anybody to know about this. You go back."

Mother did not come home, but she squatted down in the rabbit brush and watched as long as it was light enough to see. When evening came they dragged the woman to the side of the karnee, under the shelter of the windbreak, and covered her with tule mats. Mother then came home and we sat around without a fire or a light all evening. Sam forgot about being hungry and none of us ate anything until the next day. About eleven o'clock that night—anyway, it was before the roosters crowed—we heard them hitch up the wagon and load something on. It was the body of Annie Doughnuts.

The next day, Scarface Charley, when bringing a load of hay from the Lower Valley, saw a woman's head sticking out of the old emigrant well. The well had been dug by emigrants years before and had been dry for so long that it was almost filled with trash and dirt. They had dumped the witch woman in this old well and thrown only a little dirt over her. Scarface Charley recognized

Annie Doughnuts and told Bungey Jim as soon as he came to town. He asked him why he should do such a thing. That night, the wagon went out again and this time they buried her in the big sandhill below Granite Point.

When Annie Doughnuts did not show up on the second day at Hill's, they sent their son to the Indian Colony to find out what was the matter. None of the Indians would tell him anything, but the little girl, whom Annie Doughnuts had left with a couple of old Indians, said that her mother had not been home for two nights. The Hills now began to worry seriously about their missing cook.

At this time, Annie's man, Carson Charlie, was driving the stage between Bernice, a mining camp in the Clan Alpine Range, and Cottonwood Canyon, across the Dixie Valley in the East Stillwater Range. Bungey Jim and his brother knew when he would return and went several miles out to meet him. They stopped the stage in Muddlebury Canyon and told Carson Charlie not to look for his woman when he got back because they had killed her for a witch. Carson Charlie did not say a word when the Indians made this confession but got back on the stage and drove through Lovelock without stopping. He went to the Reservation ranch where the stage owner lived, took care of his team, and told him he was coming to town. Though a full-breed Paiute Indian, Carson Charlie had been raised by white people. He had never lived among the Paiutes until he was a grown man and came here. Maybe he did not believe Annie Doughnuts was a witch, for that night when he came to Lovelock he reported to the police what Bungey Jim and his sisters had done.

The next morning Eugene Couzens, the constable, Judge Aaron Brown, and a deputy came to the Indian camp about ten o'clock. We saw them coming and so did Bungey Jim's folks. Some of them started to run, and the woman who struck the killing blows tried to escape on a horse. But she did not make it. As for Bungey Jim, he lay down on the floor and began to moan and groan as if he were in awful pain. We could hear him before the officers went in the karnee. Sam and I followed the officers in and so did all the other Indians in the camp.

"Oh, me. Oh, me," groaned Bungey Jim. "Me heap sick."

"Yes," said the officer. "You look sick."

"Hand me the handcuffs," he said to the deputy. He took the handcuffs, but Bungey Jim's poor old father got between him and the constable, begging them not to take his boy.

"Bungey Jim, he heap good boy," cried the trembling old man. "He my good son, he no harm nobody." He was talking Paiute but he made himself understood with his pitiful motions. All the time, Bungey Jim was carrying on like he was dying. The men felt sorry for the old man.

"Get a rig and bring the doctor as soon as you can," said the officer. They tried to question the Paiutes but none of them knew English. Bungey Jim continued to groan.

"Annie Lowry," said Bungey Jim's wife, "you talk, you tellum Bungey Jim heap good man." I did not want to get into this.

"If you no tellum he good man," they said, "we get you next." I talked to them in pidgin English, but they did not pay me any attention. When the doctor came, Bungey Jim did extra groaning for him but it did no good. The doctor felt his pulse and listened to his heart and told the officers there was nothing the matter with Bungey Jim. They took him and three of his sisters and locked them up in jail.

After a few days, there was a trial but nobody understood anybody else.

"Did you kill'um?" the officers asked.

"Yes," the Paiutes would answer. "Me no kill'um."

"Witch woman?" they asked.

"Me no sabe," the answer came.

"Bungey Jim," the officers asked for the hundredth time, "where did you put that body?"

"I tellum you," Bungey Jim answered at last, "you no put me in jail. I put'um," he said majestically, pointing toward Granite Point, "I put'um way down." The officers took Bungey Jim and one woman down to the sand hill. Bungey Jim tried to show them where the woman was buried. This time he was not fooling—he could not find her, for a wind storm had obliterated all traces of a previous visit. They dug for two days before they found a piece of rag on a sagebrush. After digging for fifteen feet around the sage brush, they finally found the poor, fat, mangled Annie Doughnuts. They brought her body to the jail where they washed and cleaned her up.

Now they held another court but they could not make heads nor tails of the story. It was then they called me in to act as interpreter. I talked my best English this time. After they had made out a case and knew something about what had occurred, there was a regular trial at the county seat in Winnemucca. I was ordered to act as interpreter there. The Southern Pacific Railroad—the "Esspee" the Indians called it—gave free rides to all the Indians in those days, so the Paiutes went *en masse* to Winnemucca to hear the trial of Bungey Jim and his sisters.

Those Indians who were asked questions were under oath to tell the truth and nothing but the truth, but that did not mean anything to them. They would tell first one thing, then another, and there I stood, under oath also, trying to tell what they said. If I asked an Indian the lawyer's question and the witness answered it differently from what some other Indians thought he should, they would tell me not to repeat what the witness said. They talked out of turn and would answer some questions, while in response to others they would tell me to say they did not understand.

They told me they would kill me if Bungey Jim were hanged. I was not afraid of what they said, as I felt there was something higher that would protect me if I did my duty. I could have told what I knew but I figured if they did not ask me, I would not be obliged to tell. My story would have saved all the hubbub between the two races and might have changed the final sentence. But, as I said before, I was only asked to be the interpreter and that was task enough. At the end of court, Bungey Jim and two of his sisters got ten years in the state prison at Carson City. After they were in jail, the old mother used to bawl me out every time she had the chance. She thought I was the cause of Bungey Jim's being sent to prison and so did the rest of the family.

All this took place not long after I had given up my white heritage and "taken the shawl." It was all a great disappointment to learn that the Indians were as lacking in principle and right dealing as the white man. They had thought that I was good and wise when I chose to come back to them, but from the time of that trial to this good day, there has been an enmity between myself and certain

Paiutes which I have not been able to overcome.

The old mother kept telling me Bungey Jim would come back and get me but I knew he was locked up in a strong jail. When he did get out, I was married to an Indian who could protect me from any of their witchcraft.

14

MY INDIAN MARRIAGE

THE Paiute marriage customs were always strict. It was arranged between the mothers of the contracting parties and the girl was not consulted at all. The mother of the boy would suggest a certain girl for her son's wife, and if he liked the idea, his mother talked to the girl's mother. Often the son picked out the girl and asked his mother to make the arrangements. The ceremony took five days. On the night of the first day, the man slept on the outskirts of the future wife's grounds. He went home each day, but returned to sleep a little nearer his intended each night. On the morning of the fourth day, he went out to hunt and brought his day's kill for the girl to prepare and cook for him. On that night, he slept beside her bed. On the fifth day, the marriage vows were considered final. From that time on, custom decreed that he live with and care for her parents.[100]

Sanny was at our karnee a lot of the time and always brought us part of his game. I supposed he came because he was my brother-in-law, interested in his little daughter. Gradually, I began to realize that things had changed. He wanted to talk to me every time I was near him. I would not give him a chance but when he did ask me something, I would answer only "yes" or "no." Mother was always so nice to him that I knew she liked him and in her presence he never paid attention to me. I was sort of afraid of him and would not go places alone with him. As he came more often, mother began saying more nice things about him such as, "What a good worker and hunter he is," and "No one would want for food with him for a husband." One day she asked me how I would like Sanny for my husband. I told her I did not know.

"He wants me to ask you," she said. "You won't give him a chance to talk to you, and he wants me to ask you."

"Well, I don't know," I told her.

"Don't you like him?" she asked.

"I don't know," I said.

"Well, I think he would make a good husband for you," she continued. "He was so good to your sister. I want you to marry him. His mother likes you for a daughter-in-law, too."

I never would tell them if I liked Sanny, but he kept coming to the house all the time. When he went hunting, he would bring the ducks or geese to my mother instead of taking them home to his own. One day he brought several ducks and a goose, and my mother wanted me to cook for him. I sneaked out of the karnee, went through the brush, and ran to town. I did not come home until late that night and I brought a friend by the name of Mamie Joe to stay all night with me. After Mamie Joe went home the next morning, Mother said to me, "What makes you act so funny toward Sanny?" I could not say, but I knew that I did not like him and that I was afraid of him. I could never give Mother any satisfaction, but the family had been talking about us for some time.

One day, my cousin and I went to the back sloughs to get some tules for food. These grew in swampy marshes and sloughs and it was quite muddy, so we had to remove our shoes to gather them. We both started to take off our shoes when she said, "You don't have to take off your shoes. You stay here with the baby and I will go in and get the tules."

When she came back, she sat down and she put her shoes back on. We peeled the outer husk off a few of the finer tules and ate the lower end, which tastes much like bananas. This was one of our main articles of food and had been for ages back. While we were sitting there sucking and chewing the sweetness of the stems, she said to me, "Does Sanny come to your karnee all the time?"

"Yes," I answered. "But I don't like him to come there."

"Why, he is an awful nice man," said my cousin. "Don't be foolish. If he wants to marry you, marry him. We all like him and your cousin Jenny wants you to marry him, too."

So it was that all my people insisted on my being with him. They told me I could not get a better man and they were afraid I might get in with someone who would not treat me so good.

I felt kinda funny. I was a kid.[101] Mother was willing to give me up and I had no one to go to for protection. It went on like that for about six months. Then Sanny came one night just a little after sundown and stayed and stayed. Mother and I went to bed and he was still sitting there on the ground. I naturally went to sleep and I did not know whether he lay there all night but he was gone in the morning when I woke up. After Sanny began sleeping there, the girls started to tease me and to say that I was a married woman now. I never really knew until on the third night I woke up and saw a form lying about two

77

feet away from me. The next morning, Mother told me not to be silly, that if Sanny wanted to take me out and talk to me, to go with him. But I couldn't see it that way.

After I found out he had been that close to me, I began to feel like a married woman. Then, on the fourth night, I felt something touch me on the neck and I turned and found Sanny. I started fighting him and I fought like a cat. Every morning he would leave the karnee and hunt. He brought in rabbits and ducks and on the afternoon of the fourth day, when he came in, my mother wanted me to clean the game for him so she could cook it, and I did do that. On the fifth night, he lay close to me but he was not under the same covers as I was. The next day, he did not go out to hunt, and all the Paiutes congregated and told me that now I was a married woman and to behave myself and make him a good wife.

I don't think I really began to love Sanny until after the first baby was born. Before this, I never wanted to be left alone with him, and many times I was tempted to run away. If mother went out, I wanted him to go some place, too. Liking him better, a little at a time, I think it must have been four years before I loved him as a husband. I still feel that I was simply given to Sanny against my will.

For a while after we were married, we lived right there in our karnee and Sanny worked on the ranch. Then we built a bigger and better one, using the largest willows. We lived in this native house until after the first three boys were born. The first boy died there of croup. So we burned it and Sanny built a house of lumber where the rest of the children were born. The fourth boy died of cholera. Then there was a girl who died of bloody flux when she was past two years old. Then came Eva, my oldest girl, who lived. She grew up, married and had ten children, and lived in the house next to mine in the Lovelock village. Another girl died of bowel trouble. Then came the last two girls, Mabel and Sophie.

Susie worked for the Borlands, and I worked for the Prestons and Mrs. John G. Taylor. When the Indians worked for the white women regularly, each considered it as her job. If a white woman discharged her help, the other Indians would not work for her. The Indians did only the drudgery such as washing and scrubbing the floors. Though some people had a washhouse, others did their laundry out of doors, using a scrub board and boiling the clothes in a huge iron pot with three legs.

The Paiute women always took their children with them when they went to work. It was not unusual to see a Paiute woman with a papoose strapped to her back, bending over the wash tub, scrubbing the clothes. The pay was not so important as giving the family a good feed. They gave us breakfast if we were there good and early, and the dinner meal was dished up and brought out as soon as the men folks had eaten and gone back to work. If the weather was windy and cold, sometimes the washwomen were told to bring their kids into the kitchen, dish up their own food, and eat where it was warm. The Indian women were not asked to eat with the white people.

The Paiute Indians have no surnames. As a rule, they do not name their children until they are old enough to talk. Then they may name the child for some habit he has acquired, or perhaps for the first word that he spoke clearly. They like to name their girls for flowers. My second husband, Skinny Pascal, was named "Bump-head" because in a temper he used to bump his head upon the floor. Chief Winnemucca was a man not good at hunting, so he made nets and fished a great deal. One time he made a pair of shoes from his fish net. Someone saw him wearing these and called him "One-a muc-ca." "One-a" means net, and "muc-ca" means shoe. Natchez got his name because of his beautiful eyes. Dot-so-la-lee, the greatest basket maker of the Washoe people, got the first part of her name from the question, "Is that so?" She would say, "Dot so?"[102]

When the time came later that they had to use their names for signatures on papers or things of that order, the Indian men took the name of the head of the family or the party for whom he worked.[103] Sanny wanted to take the name of Holbrook, which was his adopted name, but I would not let him. Somehow I could not stand another white man's name in my family. Actually, his mother meant to call him by a pet name, "Sonny," but the way she said it, it sounded like Sanny. So Sanny became his first and also his last name. The children were given first names, and in school were known as Eva, Mabel and Sophie Sanny.

Although I was legally Mrs. Sanny, I never changed my name. After my mother and I were starving and Steve Young had arranged for Jerome Lowry to pay for what I bought at his store, I continued this charge for the support of my mother and signed the credit slips "Annie Lowry." My father did not know that I was married and had a family. We never heard from each other, and as the years went by, my signature on the Young's Store credit slip was the only reminder that he had a daughter living with the Indians in Lovelock.

One day I received a letter from my father's white wife saying that he had died, leaving her with a crippled son. She asked me to come to live with her to help take care of my half-brother. She said that she had heard that I was a strong, strapping girl and she needed me on the place. I showed the letter to Mrs. Banks for whom I then worked. She was furious. She kept the letter to answer and what she told my stepmother was plenty. My father was nearly sixty years old when he died. White friends urged me to apply for my part of his estate. They said I was legally entitled to a child's share, which I knew I was. I did not ask for one cent. I realized I would have to make a personal appearance in Oregon where he lived and where my brothers, Robert and Jackson, passed for white people, and I did not want to embarrass them. I am sure I did right.

All the old timers knew my first name was "Annie," but they spoke of me as "Annie Lowry." Newcomers, who did not know my background, hearing the full name thought it was "Annie Laurie" after the Scottish ballad. Sometimes people would say to me, "For my bonnie Annie Laurie, I would lay me down and die." Everyone then called me Annie Lowry and that is the name I used from the time when my signature was called upon.

Unlike the white women, the Paiute women had to take a back seat to their husbands. Their men were always fed first and had the choice of all the victuals. In those days, the Indians around Lovelock gambled anywhere they could find shade. One day I knew a big game was going on under the cottonwood trees back of Chinatown. On my way from work, I decided to go and watch the game. Coming by a shack, I picked up an old tin bucket to sit on while I held the baby and watched the game. Presently I felt someone kick the bucket, but I paid no attention until he shook me by the shoulders. Looking up, I saw old Mormon Dave, who had three wives, all dressed up in a white suit.

"Get up," he said. "I want that seat."

"Oh no," I told him. "I brought this seat for myself."

I'm sure that was the first time a Paiute women had the nerve to refuse to obey an Indian man in such a manner.

One time I gave a big feed for the old Indians of the tribe. My cousin from Fallon was here to help me. We had everything good to eat, including three turkeys. We cleared the front room of all the furniture and put in tables. Because Humboldt Joe and his wife were so old and nearly blind, we spread a cloth on the kitchen floor and let them eat as they were accustomed. But the others had to sit at the table. We only had half enough chairs and my cousin suggested that the women wait until the men were fed. "No," I said. "We are just as good as they are. Every chair will have to seat a man and a woman." On this occasion men and women were served and seated together at a dining table for the first time in the annals of the Paiute people.

15

YEARS OF SORROW

THE Paiutes, a nomadic tribe, traditionally buried their dead in a secret place. The body was dressed in its clothes with every ornamental trinket, necklace, and bracelet; and the deceased's loved possessions such as bows and arrows or yattahs were placed beside him. The dead person was then wrapped in his regular sleeping blankets of deer hide or animal skins. The babies were placed on cradle boards, and wrapped in their own rabbit skin blankets. Every single article belonging to the loved one was gathered up, and what could not be buried with him was burned or otherwise destroyed. The last thing done before taking the body away for burial was to set fire to the karnee in which the person died. The Paiutes took every precaution against the spirit's returning to haunt them. Next, a place was found where the body would be safe from all predatory animals, whether they traveled on two or four legs. Upon finding a suitable spot, they carefully brushed all the debris to one side in a pile. Then, following the natural contour of the land, they dug a grave. Lowering the body into it, they then placed the cooking utensils and stone grinders beside it. They filled the grave, packing it as solidly as possible. Then they scattered the debris over the grave until not a sign was left and the surrounding ground looked as if it had never been disturbed.

After the white settlers came, the Paiutes continued to hide their graves, not because of marauding animals or Indian enemies, but because of the white people. If the white people learned where a grave was, they would dig it up for curiosity or profit. Some of the bones would be sent to scientific or medical schools and the artifacts were sold to museums. I have been told some of the most valuable Indian artifacts in the Smithsonian Institute and the University of California came from this area.[104] In Lovelock, most of the graves were hidden in the surrounding sand hills.

Unwittingly, it was I who started the Indian cemetery with the burial of my son who died from a gunshot wound when he was fourteen years old. Despite my warning against playing with guns, my eldest son saved his money and without my knowledge bought one. He confided in his grandmother, Susie, who promised to keep his secret and not tell me. One morning when I was working away from home, he and some other boys decided to do some practice shooting. He climbed on a fence saying he could shoot the bullseye. As he straightened up to shoot, the gun slipped from his hand and when the butt hit the ground, it fired, and the bullet entered his body.

On that Monday morning, Sanny had gone to work, and as we had breakfast I said to Mother, "What are you going to do today?"

"Nothing," she answered, "I'm going to be at home. What are you going to do?"

"I'm going to wash for the Prestons," I said. I left and went to my work. I had separated the clothes and started to wash when here came Susie.

"I'm glad you came," I told her. "There is a big wash and you can help me."

About eleven o'clock, we had things ready and Mother was washing. While I was cleaning the lines, I saw a boy crawling over a high fence. I came back to where Mother was rubbing before the boy got there. He was wearing a white shirt and when I turned to look at him, I saw a handprint of blood on his shoulder. It was my son, Willie. "What's the matter, Son?" I asked. Willie told me that Jessie had been shot. To stop the flow of blood running down his leg, Jessie had grasped it with his hands to hold it in. Willie was trying to help him and Jessie placed his blood-stained hand on his shoulder saying, "Go tell Mother."

"Who shot him?" I asked. He told me that four of them had been playing with the gun and it slipped from his hand and discharged. I don't remember what I did, but I ran through the butcher shop and Fred Preston called to me, "What is the matter?" I did not have time to answer him. I met Jessie about half way, as he was coming to meet me.

"What have you done, my son?"

"Mother, I shot myself," he answered.

"Get on my back and I will take you home." I said. Mother told the Prestons that Jessie had been shot and then started home. The Prestons hitched their horse to the buggy and were going to take us home but I had reached there and had the boy in bed before they came.

Mr. Preston asked me how the accident happened and Jessie told him. They left to find Dr. Archer but he was in Oreana taking care of Mrs. McCarty. We had to wait until Dr. Archer came home as there were no telephones. They sent him to us as soon as he came home, which was late that night. After examining Jessie, he wired Dr. Hood to come from Battle Mountain as soon as possible as he had to have help. Through the long night, Jessie was very restless and we cried. The boy was so sorry he had not minded his mother, but he told us he was not afraid to die.

He was the most beautiful boy. The white women in Lovelock often told how good looking he was. They never forgot him. He looked like Mabel only better looking.

The next morning my white friend, Ada Springer, came and told us that Dr. Hood had arrived. She said the doctors would be there in half an hour and to take him to Dr. Archer's office to operate and try to find the bullet.

I could not bear to go inside during the operation, but his father went in and watched. He was under the anesthetic for about an hour and a half. Dr. Hood said the bullet had gone through his leg to the hip and glancing, had come back across the bowels to the liver. Sanny said the bullet wound was cut clean like a knife but they could not find the bullet. They put back the insides and sewed him up. All the Indians were waiting and when the operation was over, Ada told me it would be easier for the doctors to come to her place to see Jessie, so we took him on a stretcher to the Springers'. Sanny and I went to our Indian home to eat and came back about seven o'clock that evening. When we came in, the boy was growing restless. He was very thirsty and called to Ike,[105] who was his friend: "Partner, give me some water." Ike brought him a glass but Mrs. Springer told him he could not have it yet. When he saw me crying, he said, "Don't cry, Mother. I did not mind you, so I will have to die. I do not mind dying."

"I know, son, but I do not want you to suffer." I told him.

"The clouds are opening now. Good-bye." He threw out his hands, one to me and one to Sanny who was on the opposite side of the bed. That was the last of our Jessie.

After Jessie's death, there was a great emptiness in our house. Our grief was so great that we failed to notice that his dog, Puppy, was gone. When we finally missed him, we looked everywhere and we found him in a couple of days lying beside Jessie's grave. We took him home and tried to get him to eat something but he just sat and whimpered. When our backs were turned, he was gone again and we learned that from then on we would find him in the same place, beside the grave. This went on for several weeks until we had to kill him as he would eat nothing and became so weak he could not stand. We always felt that their spirits were together in the happy hunting ground.

Jessie, my firstborn, was the shining light in my mother's eyes. He was very good to Susie, and he loved her very much. She would tell him tales and taught him many things. When he died, something died in my mother, too. She blamed herself for Jessie's death and told us that she was the one who was in the wrong for letting Jessie have the gun without my knowledge, and that he would not be gone if she had told me about it. Her appetite was gone and she would sit around looking into space. As the weeks went on, you could see her becoming more frail each day. We tried to get her to see the doctor but she said she did not want that. She told us that she wanted to die and be with Jessie. Two months after we lost our Jessie, my mother passed quietly away.[106]

Sanny took sick in the summmer of 1909. I sent for the white doctor to come and see him. He continued sick for weeks. Finally, the doctor told us Sanny had walking typhoid, that he had passed the limit and was too far gone for anything to be done for him. He ran terrible fevers night and day. At night especially, when the fever would be very high, he would go into delirium and talk the whole night through. The Paiutes believe when a sick person talks in delirium, his soul has gone to the happy hunting grounds and he is talking to his ancestors. For some reason, he is kept on this earth to pay for past wrongdoing. If this delirium continues for any length of time, the Paiutes think it is their duty to assist the spirit to leave. Usually the easiest way to do this is by smothering.[107] I could not bear to think of doing this to Sanny and as the days went by I became obsessed with the fear that when I was away or asleep, someone would perform this act. So for days on end, I alone took entire care of my husband. During the day, his delirium seemed to allow him restless sleep, but at night when his fever was higher, he groaned and screamed and showed amazing strength. I was afraid to sleep soundly for all those months before Sanny died in January of 1910.

Because of a heavy snowfall, we were unable to bury Sanny right away. We moved to a neighbor's vacant house and lived there until I could afford to move ours to another lot and change the windows and doors. Sanny's mother refused to go with us but stayed in the kitchen of the house where Sanny was until after the funeral. She then went to live with her daughter, Coffee Charley's wife, in Fallon.

I must have been on the verge of collapse. I couldn't cry, my body was worn to skin and bones, there was no food for the children, and I had only fifteen cents to my name. When my son, Willie, realized how poor we were, he went to Carpenter's ranch and sold his one and only calf and brought me the money. I knew how much the boy thought of the calf and the sacrifice he had made for his mother. I broke down and cried for the first time since Sanny died.

About this time, Rosie Lee, her sister, and her mother contracted smallpox from the white people in Lovelock. Authorities quarantined the entire Indian village. Never since the white man came to this country did a band of Paiutes have such a good time as during the weeks of the smallpox quarantine. None of them was very sick from this disease and no one else contracted it. But no one was allowed to leave the camp and there was nothing to do for three weeks. One member of the family would stand in line each day to get the food which was cooked and ready to eat when the white people brought it. I was too sick with grief and worry to stand. My daughter, Eva, had to get our family's share. In their idleness they played Indian gambling games and revived games their forebears had played in ancient times. The stick and rag game was the one that gave them the most enjoyment.

The game is much like hockey, but a rag is used instead of a puck. The "rag" is made by braiding cloth, making it hard and about eight inches long with a knot at each end. The stick is a willow, wider at the striking end. The ground is marked off with a goal at each end, and captains choose sides. The object is to get the rag over the opponent's goal. Everyone played. They gambled with everything they had, even their clothes. They had apples which had been sent to be distributed equally, but only the winners ate apples. They gambled on the number of strikes to make a goal and on the final result of the games. All the men were on one side and the women on the other. Sometimes they played wild. The women would run for the goal but fall down on the way. The men would try to hit them with the rag before they got up. The women would laugh even if it hurt and would jump up and run some more.[108] Eva watched these games while standing in line and when she came home, would describe the high old times the people were having. I could hear them laughing and shouting. The laughter was more contagious than the smallpox. Through hearing their merriment, a little joy seeped into my system and with good food and plenty of sleep, I began to feel better and put on weight. By the time the quarantine was lifted, I was almost my normal self again.

We buried Sanny near the graves of Jessie and my mother. Other members of our tribe began burying their dead near this same place. It is now known as the Lovelock Indian Cemetery. I wanted to place headboards to identify where my loved ones were buried, so I designed them and asked my son-in-law to help me. He cut them out from heavy boards and painted them white with a black border around each and put the names and the dates in large black lettering. He then took me in the old spring wagon, pulled by one horse, and I placed them where they belonged. After they were finished, I turned to my son-in-law and said, "My, they are beautiful. Nothing you could have done would have made me as happy."[109]

16

MY SON WILLIE

INDIANS go by signs more than the white people do, and more of them have signs come to them than the white people—although some of both races do not have them at all. When I was young, I did not believe in the Indians' signs, nor in magic. But during the pinenut season many years ago, something happened to change my view of mystical things.

One beautiful day in the late fall, Sanny suggested we leave the children with old lady Sanny and go to the East Range to gather pinenuts. I had been sick all summer, just dragging around, and he thought it would do me good to get away from the children, out in the open country. We hitched the horses to the wagon, threw in camping things, and Mother, Jessie, his dog, Puppy, and I started for pinenuts. After we set up camp with another family who had come for the same reason, we started out to get the cones. Mother, Jessie, and I separated from Sanny and the rest of the party who crossed a knoll and went in another direction. We found the nut trees and were filling a ka-wan[110] when the little dog began to bark. We looked across the valley and saw what we thought was another pinenutting party. There was a woman in a pink dress, a man and a boy, a little dog, and a horse loaded with camping gear. We filled our ka-wans and started back to camp but I could not carry anything because I was so weak I could hardly walk. Mother was so loaded she could not help me. I staggered along, stopping often to rest. Finally I had to crawl into camp. We were so tired and worn we could not get food for ourselves, so we just waited until the others came to do the evening work. After we had eaten, we told them about seeing the group of people in the valley. They had seen no one, but one woman said their little dog had barked and she had told it to shut up. When it continued to bark, she kicked it for barking at nothing. She was sorry she had kicked the poor little thing. They said the party we saw must have been Mustache Charley and his family who were to join them that evening. They did not come, and we could see no campfire that night. The next morning we went to the place where we had seen the three people, the dog, and the horse. There was no trace of human beings or animals to be found. We talked it over and decided that the strange vision, apparition, mirage, or whatever it was, was a sign that something was going to happen to some of our party. Mustache Charley believed this, too. He said something told him not to leave his karnee that day, although he had planned to go and had told people that was his intention. True enough, three of our party died before the new year came, an old man, my mother, and Jessie. Since that strange appearance in the valley, I believe in signs and I am careful not to ignore them.

The Indian doctor or the medicine man has great powers to work with the spirits to heal the sick. When my second son, Willie, was three years old, he had a spell of some kind of sickness and we sent for Coffee Charley, the

Indian doctor. We knew Willie was passing and the father told Coffee Charley how he was acting and the doctor said he could help him. We were all out of doors by the campfire and the child was with us lying on the ground. The boy was stiffened, just exactly as if he were dead. The doctor told us he would go into a trance, that he would lie down, and for us to place the child beside him. He told us to watch very carefully, and when he, the doctor, was coming out of the trance he would move and we must see whether the boy moved, too. If he did, then he was coming back; if not . . . we did not talk about that. For a long time we sat with our minds on the coming back of our son. Then the doctor moved an arm. The boy moved an arm. Then the body of the doctor shook all through, and the boy's body seemed to shudder. Coffee Charley opened his eyes and the eagle feather in his hand stood straight up. He told us to raise him to a sitting position. He asked if the boy had moved and we told him yes. Then he touched the boy. "Come on, child," he said, "we are coming home to mother." He asked us to help him to his feet and as he stood over the boy with the eagle feathers in his hand, which were two feathers fastened to a stick, he sang this song: "A baby was spared by the Great Spirit and was sent home to its mother." As he sang, repeating the words many times, he gently moved the hand holding the feathers over the child's body. Finally, the feathers began to move. When they were at right angles, one pointing straight up and the other poised over the child's body, the child said, "Mama."

"Speak to him, Sister," said the doctor.

"Son, oh, my child, come to Mother."

It was a moving scene by the campfire. All of us had

tears in our eyes. But when his father started to pick him up, he was still stiff, just as stiff as a board. Coffee Charley told us he would be all right, for us to take good care of him and when he was himself again, to find a clean pool of water to bathe him in. Willie improved right along, and a week later, he seemed entirely well.[111]

Son Willie grew to be a man in the Indian village. He had no education and no trade. He never smoked or drank. He was good looking and strong—a perfect physical specimen of manhood. He was only about fifteen when Sanny died, but he took the responsibility of raising his three little sisters like a man. He never wanted them to do anything wrong. When he came from work, if they were not at home, he would ask where they were and insist that they come in before dark.

The show-house was next to the Park Hotel. He took his sisters to nearly every picture and often invited me to join them. We never missed a Charlie Chaplin show because we knew his leading lady, Edna Purviance, who was a former Lovelock girl. I worked for her sister, and Edna was often around the house. The audience used to cheer when she came on the screen.

Although he had no schooling, he wanted the sisters to receive an education and he saw to it that Eva, the eldest, attended Stewart Indian School near Carson City for three years. He paid for her education by playing baseball in Lovelock.

When he was twenty-one, he married a Paiute girl by the name of Annie Donnely. We lived as neighbors on the same lot. They had no children and Annie started to run around, and when Willie would come home from work he would ask me where she was. That went on for quite a while and one evening he came over and had very little to say.

"Is Annie home?" I asked.

"No, and she is not going to be home. I have put a stop to her acting the way she does. I will not put up with her foolishness any longer."

That night Annie came home about eleven o'clock and knocked on the door, but he would not let her in. She came over to our place and I let her in and she slept there that night. The next morning, I did not ask her anything but I gave her breakfast and then I went to work. The following evening, she met Willie in town and asked him why he did not open the door. He told her that he was not going to have her come home at all times of the night and he did not want her to come home anymore—that he was through with her.

"You can't blame me. Alice did not want to come home," she said. Alice was an orphan girl who lived with Annie's mother.

"If you think more of Alice than you do me, you had better stay with her," he said. Later he came to me and said, "Mother, next time she comes to the door, do not let her in. She can go to her own mother's." Her mother lived across the street from us.

Two years after that, he married a girl by the name of Norma Robinson, part Shoshone, from Winnemucca. They lived in the same house where he had lived with Annie Donnely, and had two little girls named Elsie and Helen. It was then that he took up baseball, playing with the white boys in town. He could play any position on the team, but pitching was his best. He was offered a position in the big leagues, but he did not want to be away from

95

his family. I knew his education was so poor that he would be unable to cope with the white race in a large city, so I discouraged him.

One evening, when supper was ready, the wife said there was no sugar in the house. He jumped on his horse bareback and rode into town to the Azores store. Besides the sugar, he bought two cans of fruit. When he started home, he had his arms full of bundles and made his horse go into a lope. He had just started when his horse slipped and fell. Willie was thrown over his head and he lit on his side on top of the cans of fruit that had rolled from the bag. When Willie reached home, he came in and said, "There's the sugar and besides I am hurt." It was not long after that his side began to bother him. In spite of the pain, he still pitched hay and did shoveling. It was so severe that at times he could not work. He went on like that for two years and I told him to go to Dr. Smith and find out what was causing it, but he said he would be alright.

Willie remembered the Indian doctor had cured him when he was small. He asked me about going with him to Nixon to get help from him. He had a car and he and his family and I drove to Nixon. When Coffee Charley came to treat Willie, he was wearing a blue shirt, overalls, and Indian moccasins. Around his neck he wore a bear-claw necklace. He had a band, made of buckskin with an eagle feather stuck in it, around his head. Two eagle feathers were in his right hand. He sat down among us and asked Willie where he was ailing. Coffee Charley told him to lie on his back so he could doctor him. He passed the eagle feathers over him slowly, back and forth, until they seemed to tremble over the area where the pain was. He said, "You are pretty bad off. You have a big lump under your ribs. I can do nothing for you now, but tomorrow night I will doctor you."

We stayed there all the next day and a crowd of Indians came to the camp, which was still made up of old tule karnees. About eight o'clock the doctor came and started to treat him. First, he started to sing a song. Then he had the medicine pipe filled with Indian tobacco and this he passed with his right hand across his body to the next man on his left, who took one smoke and passed it on to the next one in the same fashion until it was returned to the doctor. After the smoking was over, he got on his knees beside Willie and opened his clothing over the pain in his side. Lowering his head, he began sucking on Willie's side and then spitting. He went through all sorts of motions, as though he were spitting out the disease. He continued this until about midnight. "I can get no message from the Great Spirit," he said. "I will go into a trance and see what I can do for you." This he did, and became so stiff they could not bend an arm or leg. While he was in this condition, the rest of the Indians sang songs and swayed their bodies from side to side. When he began making a queer noise, they knew he was coming from his trance. They tried to raise him up but he was so stiff it was like picking up a dead man. There was an old Indian man there who told them not to try to bend his limbs for fear of breaking them, and to get the eagle feathers. They put a feather under each knee and gradually bent them, then they used them under the elbows. After getting these bent, too, they took the feathers and laid them across the waistline and he was able to sit up. It was about ten minutes before he could talk. Then he said, "My boy, I can't do anything for you. None of the things that grow will cure you. I am sorry you cannot be cured through my power. Maybe another doctor with more power than I have can do something for you, but I do not know where you will find him."[112]

The next day, we came home and went to see Dr. Smith. He told us that the bruise from the fall from the horse two years before had caused an enlargement of the spleen. A few days later, Willie died peacefully, just like a child going to sleep.

17

JOHN PASCAL

WHEN a woman is faced with the responsibility of supporting a family alone, then she begins to appreciate what it means to have a man who works. With the help of relatives and friends, our house where my husband died was changed and moved to another lot where we lived until the government gave us land for our Indian village. We then moved it to the present location and have lived here ever since.

Realizing my urgent need, well-meaning friends advised me to give my children away or to send them to the government Indian orphanage. Several families wanted to adopt them and one couple was so anxious for a daughter they offered me a settlement which would have eased my financial burden for years. But I could not bear to part with any of my children. I was determined to keep my family together and give them a normal, happy life.

To make ends meet, I worked every angle. Willie, who should have been in school, went to work at Carpenter's ranch. Eva was old enough to stay with the little girls or help when I took them with me to work. Instead of working at my two steady jobs two days a week as was my habit, I now doubled up, finishing one by dinner time and going to another in the afternoon. When I could get them, I took two jobs a day every day of the week. I baked fresh bread for Willie and his friends when they came in from the ranch. Besides making clothes for the girls and myself, I took in sewing which I did by lamplight after the children were in bed.

Busy all day and far into the night, I never had time to go places or to visit except with a few friends who came to the house and talked to me while I cooked, cleaned, or sewed. The young Indians who came from work on the ranch with Willie were always hungry and lively. They kept me more or less informed about what was going on among the Paiutes. They confided their love affairs to me and I never betrayed their secrets. One day they told me seriously that scouts had been here and told them that very soon there was going to be an Indian uprising in which all of them would have to take part. The Paiutes and Shoshones together had planned a series of raids on the ranches and towns all along the Humboldt River.

Shocked by the import of this terrible news, the next two days, I think, were the longest and most miserable of my life. Under the pledge of secrecy I could not discuss it with others. If I should warn the white men, all the Indians would be in trouble. I felt that raids were the worst form of war.

When the boys came from the fields on the second day, they brought good news. John S. Pascal, an English-speaking Paiute, had talked to the leaders of both tribes. He explained the uselessness of such an uprising. He showed them that burning the fields and destroying property would hurt the Indians more than the whites. He had persuaded them to signal the communities to call off the raids.

Oh, what a relief! My heart felt as if it would burst with gratitude to this man who, working with the white people, was a true friend of the Indian. His action had saved both races from terrible bloodshed and pillage. John Pascal, I said to myself, must be "Skinny" Pascal, the friend of the U.S. Government who helped settle and make peace after the great uprising in 1876. He must be the same fellow who went with my cousin, Jenny Harris, when we lived in Winnemucca. I remembered him as slim, good-looking, and full of fun. I wondered how he had learned to speak such good English. It seems most of his youth had been spent with white people in northwestern Nevada near Fort McDermitt. He was very friendly with the soldiers stationed there. They hired him to track and bring back their stolen horses. The sheriff also called upon him to track criminals. They bragged about him a lot and said he could track anything the law was after.[113]

I had not seen Pascal since Mother and I made our hasty exit from Winnemucca years before, although I knew he married one of Bungey Jim's daughters who had died leaving him with two children, William and Rosie, who now lived with their grandmother here in the Indian village. I still pictured him as a gay young man of twenty years ago. Thoughts of him constantly flooded my mind as I did my daily work and I happily relived every occasion I had had in his company. Some time after the threatened uprising, Pascal came to the Lovelock Indian village to live.

When he first came to the house, a mature, middle-aged man, I could not adjust my mental image of him to his physical appearance, until it dawned on me that time had stood still only in my mind. When we shook hands a current of mutual understanding seemed to pass between us that bridged the years. It was as if two young people met and fell in love at first sight.

After that first meeting, Pascal was among the friends who often dropped in to chat while I did my housework. So casual were his visits that neither the neighbors nor any of the family suspected that we were in love. When I told the children they were going to have a new papa, they were tickled to death. The youngest girls were such babies when their father died they did not remember him at all. They wanted a father and thought it would be grand to have Pascal's children for brother and sister.

Before we were married, Pascal promised never to touch my children by way of punishment. I felt that it was my duty to take care of that chore. He kept his word and never laid a hand on them. He taught them and guided them as a wise father should, and they loved him in return as much as if he had been their own.

Pascal declared he tried to marry me in Winnemucca. "This gal," he would say to whoever was listening, "was my sweetheart when we were young."

"That's not so," I broke in.

"I wanted to marry you then," he said.

"You didn't ask me," I answered.

"You wouldn't give me a chance," he said. "Why was that?"

"You were going with my sister," I told him. "I wouldn't take her fellow away from her."

My cousin Jenny was jealous of me in those days. I always wondered why until this joking conversation. Then it flashed through my mind. She had been jealous because she knew Pascal was in love with me.

Pascal and I were very congenial. We had both associated with white people and spoke English naturally. Yet we believed in the Indian way of life. He was as smart as they come. About business and handling people, he reminded me of my white father, but he had never learned to read. When I realized how much he longed to read, I taught him how. He was an apt pupil and in his later years he enjoyed reading the newspapers very much.

Upon our marriage, Pascal built an addition to the house. This was to be our room. It was nice and comfortable, with large outside windows and a door that opened on the front yard. I stopped working out and he took the responsibility of providing for the family. While he was still on call at all times as a tracker, he was also a seasonal worker. In the summer he worked as a hay-hand on the ranches. In winter he fed cattle and sheep. His speciality was sheep shearing and in the spring his crew of ten or twelve trained men, picked from all over the country, met him in Winnemucca. From there they went from one big sheep corral to another, shearing all the bands in range of each. He took care of the animals of John G. Taylors' interests, and only Pascal could shear his prize bucks. I went along with the outfit, and I was the camp tender and cook. We made a rule to take a month's vacation between sheep shearing and haying. We called it our time to be free. We went where we liked, did what we pleased, and returned rejuvenated in mind and body.

Every year the Indians take their families to the hills to gather pinenuts, just as they have done for ages. When Pascal was head man in the village, it was he who had to go before the middle of August and scout to find out the conditions of the trees, and see if the nuts were plentiful or scarce and bring back a few cones and call a powwow. All the Indians of the village come for the ceremony. Men, women, and children dance in a circle. The chief or head man of the village stands in the center of the big circle and offers thanks to the Big Man for the nuts they had last year, and asks in prayer for a better crop this year. Then they begin their dance, again in a circle. The chief gives out the cones to men who test them for quality and ripeness. They know from this test how many days before they should go out to gather the pinenuts. This is almost always the first week of September. The pinenut powwow ceremony usually lasts all night. But if the Paiutes decide that the crop looks poor and there will not be enough pinenuts for the people, they break two or three pinenut cones, put them in water, and dance two or three nights— sometimes even an entire week. The season for picking pinenuts lasts for three weeks or until the first heavy frost.

We followed this way of living, more or less, for many years, until one day Pascal's team was frightened and ran away. Mabel and I were at home and saw the horses rear back on their hind legs with their front feet pawing the air. They started to run and left the village road and tore past our house. Pascal was thrown into the ditch and the wagon passed over his body. When we picked him up, we carried him to our room. We found him so seriously injured that he never walked again without the aid of crutches. Pascal did not believe in doctors so I took care of him. One time we went to Nixon and he was treated by a new kind of Indian doctor. The man was a faddist and popular for only a short time. He rubbed Pascal and gave him some herb pills which he concocted himself. After three weeks we came home to our comfortable home and I continued the treatment there. He was able to be up and about, visiting with his many friends in the village, and he read a lot. We would often sit and talk about the beliefs of our ancestors. He seemed to fade gradually away until one evening he looked at me and said, "Annie, I think this is it." He turned his head toward the setting sun and quietly passed away. After he was buried, we tore off the one room that meant so much to us, and I moved back into the rest of the original house.

The Paiutes believe in heaven but they do not know anything about hell. We are taught that we go to heaven when we die. Being good or bad has nothing to do with it. I know we get our hell on earth, but we are not taught that in our religion. We are taught that the Big Man is in heaven ready to receive our souls and we do not think of any punishment. We believe that we will meet our loved ones in that next world and we will know them and they will know us. In fact, we will know anyone whom we have previously known on earth. About spirits returning, that seldom occurs. When in a trance, the Indian doctor has been known to enter the spirit world, but a common person can not. The Indian doctors have great power to heal and cure people. This power comes from the Big Man, who tells them how to make sick people well. Those men are called by the Great Spirit, and it is He who tells them what to do.[114] The younger generation does not have such power.[115]

18

POSTLUDE

Eighteen years before her death, Annie Lowry suffered a stroke and was paralyzed. This is the story of her healing as related by her daughter, Eva.

I SAW with my own eyes the cure by an Indian doctor, and nothing in my life stays with me like that healing. It was wonderful. If the white people could have watched that, they would know that the Indian doctor had the power.[116] Mamma came in from work one day—I think she had been washing at Mrs. Heizer's—anyway she said she was tired, and the next morning she could not see out of one eye. She did not try to work and we sent for Dr. West. We doctored with him for awhile but Mamma got no better although he came every day.

One day, a white friend, Mrs. Taylor, came down and told us she was going to take Mamma to Reno to the hospital. At St. Mary's they gave her a good going over. They could not find anything the matter with her. They X-rayed her, I guess, all over—you ought to have heard Mamma tell all they did to her. But they could not find anything wrong. She was paralyzed on one side and could hardly see from either eye now. She heard the doctors and nurses talk and say she would never get well and also that she was crazy. They did not know she could hear every word they said.

Mamma waited until they left her. She got a friend who worked in the hospital to get her clothes and help her get dressed. Somehow she managed to get downstairs where the sisters told her she could not leave and tried to take her back to bed. She was such a big woman, the sisters could not handle her.

Of course we were worried about Mamma, but we did not know she was so sick. It is strange, but that was the day that Mabel and Sophie picked to go on the train to Reno to visit her. They went directly to Mamma's room where the nurses told them she was waiting for them downstairs. In her condition, the nurses were amazed at how she had dressed and managed to get downstairs. When Mamma saw the girls she told them what the doctors had said and begged them to take her home. She said if she was going to die, as the doctors had said, she wanted to die at home. It was only a few minutes until train time, and they called a taxi and the hospital aides helped her. The train was ready to pull out when they reached the station. Mabel told the conductor their predicament. He understood and held the train until she could buy the tickets and then helped them put Mamma on the train. The sisters wired Mrs. Taylor that Mamma had left St. Mary's. When they got to Lovelock, Mickey Cawley, the constable, and Mr. Randolph met the train and brought Mamma home. By this time, she did not know anyone, her teeth were chattering, and she could not see at all.

Willie, my brother, was pitching hay with the Indian doctor, George Calico, down on Carpenter's ranch. Willie was talking to him about Mamma's being so sick, and the doctor said he would like to treat her. He said she was too young to die, that he might not be able to cure her, but he wanted to try. When Willie came home that night he told us sisters what the Indian doctor had said. The family talked it over and decided we would have him treat her.

Only certain people can talk to the Indian doctor and we got our cousin, Ben Charley, who knew how to do it and what to say. He had to go and talk to him just before the sunrise. He said he would do what he could for Mamma and gave Ben Charley a willow stick with two eagle feathers tied to it. One feather is the longest in the eagle's tail, the other is a short fluffy one from under the tail. We put the stick in a bucket of dirt and placed it at the head of Mamma's bed so it could wave all day above her head. Nobody was allowed to touch the feathers.

After working all day in the field, the Indian doctor came and started his cure at seven o'clock. Mamma had to be put on the floor, and it took four men to place her there, for she was such a big woman. He started working her head, giving it a massage for almost half an hour, then he stopped and would sing. The neighbors came in and watched, and everyone there joined in the singing. He sang the most beautiful songs, then he massaged again. We had to give Mamma clean handkerchiefs often, for she seemed to blow her nose and spit lots. Alternating the massage and the singing, he worked until twelve o'clock— not before twelve nor after, but exactly at twelve. We had a little lunch prepared—well, it was a big lunch—cakes, roast, salad, mashed potatoes, and coffee. The doctor would smoke a little and rest besides eating food. Then he started massaging and singing again. About two o'clock, he told us what was the matter with her. He said she had

a clot on the brain. He kept up the massage and the singing until sunrise the next day. He told Willie to cut a good
strong willow stick, one Mamma could use for a walking
stick. He told him to fix it up nice and to hide it in
Mamma's room. She was to know nothing about this.

Willie cut the stick and hid it in the closet. Next morning, when we got Mamma on the bed and cleaned up, we
found the handkerchiefs she had blown her nose on were
pink with bloody streaks on them. We were awfully scared
of that blood but did not say anything. We were afraid
we would break the spell or kill the power. That day she
was better and could eat. The second night, the doctor
came and went through the same routine as on the first
night, massaging her and singing at regular intervals.

The third night, he told us to get five rocks out of the
water.[117] They must be clean rocks, not to come from
dirty water. Willie went to the river over by Ruddel's
ranch, where he could wade in fresh water, and got the
rocks. They had to be placed against the wall opposite
Mamma's bed, beginning in the northeast corner, a few
feet apart, equidistant. At intervals during the day, say at
nine, eleven, and so on, the rocks were moved, one at a
time. About five, the fourth rock was moved. The rock left
in the corner was moved exactly at sunset. We had Sister
watch from the west window to say when, and then we
moved it. We knew that it made no difference how far the
rock was moved—that it need only be picked up and set
down again.

On the fourth night, exactly the same procedure was
followed. Each day we picked up a rock, one every day
until the fifth day, then we took the five rocks to the river
and put them where they came from.

On the morning of the fifth day I came from my house,

just twenty feet away, and entered Mamma's house through the kitchen. I opened the door into her room, and I could not believe what I saw. In the doorway stood Mamma, who only days before had been paralyzed! There she stood. She had the cane in her hand and was watching the sunrise. Mamma, who had been helpless for weeks and was blind, standing in the door, watching the sunrise. "Mamma, Mamma. What is the matter? Sit down."

I dragged her old rocker up and she sat down. I got slippers for her bare feet and she looked up at me and smiled. I got her breakfast, and after several hours she let us help her to bed. Every day she improved, and began again to do her work. She lived for eighteen years afterward. She never could tell us how she got up or remembered where she found the cane.

COMMENTARY

BY CHARLES R. CRAIG

The Northern Paiutes, with whom this story is concerned, now occupy an area which approximates that which they inhabited at the time of their first contact with the white man. This area, which in shape resembles that of the continent of South America, nearly covers the western half of Nevada, and spills over into three neighboring states. At its sourthern extremity, it extends into California to Owens Lake; the western boundary then follows the Sierra Nevada northward, veering eastward into Nevada around Carson City and Reno, back into California, then northward again and over the boundary into Oregon, where it reaches Malheur Lake, its northern extremity. Thence it arcs across the western boundary of Idaho and curves southeastward until it intersects the northern boundary of Nevada slightly east of its midpoint, and drops south in the vicinity of Battle Mountain and Austin and continues down and across the slanting California state line to Owens Lake once again.

To speak of a Paiute "tribe" is misleading, for the term implies a concentration, homogeneity, and political unity which did not exist. The Paiutes moved about in bands, often widely separated, under the leadership of individuals who probably derived their authority by virtue of their ability to find food or from their natural position as the head of a family, not from hereditary privilege. This should not imply that the Paiutes did not feel a sense of identity with those of other bands, but only that their primary identity was with the family or the local band rather than with any centralized authority or "chief." (When, under pressure of white civilization, certain leaders, such as Winnemucca, made agreements and treaties affecting the Paiutes, their ability to enforce the agreements depended upon the moral influence they exerted over their followers. Their power did not derive, as the white leaders sometimes assumed, from any established political authority as we understand it.) The Paiutes cannot, then, be defined as a political or semipolitical entity, but simply as a group of people who shared certain cultural, religious, and linguistic similarities by which they identified themselves and each other.

To the early trappers, explorers, and emigrants, all the Indians of the area west of the Wasatch Mountains were "diggers," so called because much of their time was spent in grubbing for food-roots and rodents. The term, which was generally derogatory, implied the lack of any distinctive traits that might distinguish one group of Indians from another and ignored the real differences which did exist. The Indians themselves were more discriminating, and while they were usually too busy to trouble themselves about their distant neighbors, they were aware of the differences between them. To the west of the Paiutes lay the Sierra Nevada range, which effectually separated them from the bands of California Indians that inhabited the Pacific slopes. The peaks were passable in the summer, and some trading parties crossed over, but the deep winter snows prevented sustained contact between the two. Of more concern to the Paiutes were the Washoes who lived in the vicinity of Lake Tahoe and with whom they frequently quarreled. The Paiutes also told of battles with Indians in northern California, but this hostility seems to have been traditional, perhaps mythical, rather than historical. To the northeast, in Idaho, lived the Bannocks, and to the east, the Shoshones. The Southern Paiutes, who occupied the southern tip of Nevada, are misnamed, for they are of an entirely different ethnic group than the Northern Paiutes. It should be understood that the boundaries thus delineated were of little importance in themselves; they did not in any real sense exist in areas too desolate to support a population, and became significant only when they intersected or neared food-gathering areas important enough to cause contention. Moreover, even in populated areas, cultural boundaries were more complex than we have implied. Neighboring Indians traded with one another and often intermarried, or an individual Shoshone might live in peace with a band of Paiutes. Consequently, in many marginal areas Indians of different stock shared many common cultural characteristics.

The Paiutes' failure to capture the popular imagination is not surprising, considering their peaceful nature, the simplicity of their culture, and their lack of elaborate ceremony. They boasted no warriors as did the plains tribes, nor did they weave colorful blankets, make pottery, or practice elaborate ceremonial dances as did the Indians of the southwest. The barrenness of northwestern Nevada forced its inhabitants to follow a way of life that was more practical than spectacular. Aside from occasional squabbles over food-gathering areas with the neighboring Washoes and Shoshones, the Paiutes did not practice warfare and therfore attached little importance to the war-

rior. Instead, honor lay in an individual's ability to provide food, for economics in the Great Basin were harsh,
and starvation awaited those who were lazy or inept. In
matrimony, the woman was chosen for her strength and
her energy, and the man courted her by demonstrating his
prowess as a hunter. Large animals were scarce, and aside
from an occasional antelope or mountain sheep, the
Paiutes depended on rabbits, ground squirrels, and other
small rodents for their meat. Waterfowl and fish from the
marshes and lakes constituted another source of food, but
for the most part, the Indians lived on mush made from
grass seeds and pinenuts gathered from the valleys and
the hillsides. As is often the case in barren lands, poverty
begat generosity, and no one was ever denied food by
those who had it.

Because few areas could long sustain any sizable number of Indians, the Paiute bands were forced to wander
constantly from one place to another. These seasonal mi-
grations in search of food inhibited the development of
public ritual, and most religious observations were individual affairs. Every man was his own priest and observed
a system of taboos to avoid offending the many powerful
spirits which surrounded him. But if for some reason the
spirits were offended and someone became ill, his family
summoned an Indian doctor, a member of the band to
whom the spirits had given the power to heal sickness.
The simple but impressive healing ritual constituted one
of the few important public religious observances. The
doctor usually worked for the benefit of the community
and was a respected member of it, but occasionally one
was accused of being a sorcerer who used his power not
to cure disease, but to cause it, and unless he was able to
disprove the charge, he was executed for the good of the

band. Thus, almost every aspect of Paiute culture was concerned with the well-being, physical and spiritual, of the individual or the community.

With the coming of the white man, the Indian culture was permanently and drastically changed. The Great Basin was, aside from the polar regions, the last part of the North American continent to be explored, and during this time there was a great discrepancy between the values of the two races. As long as the white men and the Indians existed independently of one another this difference was of little significance to either. During the period between 1828 and 1848, bands of trappers, explorers, and emigrants were to be seen along the Humboldt River, but they were few and most of them were gone before winter. In 1849, the gold rush brought more than twenty thousand emigrants along the river, and with them came sixty thousand head of stock that stripped the valley floors of the food-grasses which grew there. But still, the intrusion lasted only from midsummer to mid-September, when the last wagons passed, and the Paiutes were at least partially compensated for the loss of their grasses by the horses and cattle which they stole from the emigrant camps.

It was not until the discovery of silver in Nevada that the white culture came into direct conflict with that of the Indians. The people who flocked to Virginia City in 1859 and to the Humboldt in 1861 were no longer emigrants, hurrying to cross the Sierra, but settlers. The few fertile areas, that before had precariously supported a few thousand Indians, soon teemed with white men. The food-grasses became mule-fodder and the nut-pines were cut for fuel. After an exceptionally severe winter, the Indians' resentment erupted into a series of battles which sputtered intermittently through the sixties, but resistance came too late, for they were then outnumbered. Their only coordinated attempt to drive out the whites was obscured by the events leading to the outbreak of the Civil War in the East and has been all but ignored by history. The Paiutes did not have the option of retreat, for there was no place for them to go. If unburdened by a family, an Indian was able to survive in the desert longer than could a white man, but no band of any size could exist there indefinitely. Consequently, the only avenue left was that of acculturation, or some degree of it. Some Paiute bands lived and languished on badly managed reservations, and others learned to work for their new masters. A few were willing to hunt down and kill bands of recalcitrants and as a result, bred enmities that lasted for generations. In more peaceful times they served as guides or worked as laborers on ranches. Perhaps in one way the new life was beneficial, for the white civilization was never without food, and the Indians who lived on its fringes were no longer so dependent upon the caprice of nature.

As the Indian culture changed, an ambiguous relationship developed between the Indian and the white man—a relationship seldom touched upon in formal studies of history or anthropology. Articles dealing even generally with these groups are confined to scholarly journals and are often couched in terms that the layman finds discouraging.[118] Besides the historical interest of this narrative, then, direct depiction of the relationship that has existed between the Indian and the white man for the last hundred years has value even when direct documentation is difficult to confirm.

We find evidence that the Paiutes showed themselves quite willing to make adjustments to the demands of civilization. For instance, age-old custom dictated that when someone died, his family was obliged to burn his hut to prevent the return of his spirit. But when the government undertook to provide houses for the Indians, it forbade them to continue such an extravagant practice. This, of course, posed a delicate problem, for as much as they liked their new homes, the Indians thought ghosts more real and at times considerably more dangerous than a bureaucracy that generally ignored them. But the Paiutes had always been an eminently sensible and practical people, and satisfied both the spirits and the government by simply changing about the doors and windows or moving the house a few feet off its original foundation.

Unfortunately, the problem of acculturation was not always solved so easily, particularly when the white people did not find it convenient. Jerome Lowry, like other white men of the era, took his Indian wife[119] at a time when the Humboldt area was little more than a wilderness, and women of any race were a rarity. Later, when his own circumstances had improved and he could afford to be more discriminating, he found that his wife had become an embarrassment and he deserted her with as little thought as he had used when he married her. In the same way, the white settlers were happy enough to use the Indian as a source of cheap labor, but made no effort to prepare him to take a place in the modern world. Nor did they feel any obligation to do so, for that was the government's responsibility. Unfortunately, the government failed miserably.

Locally, the white community adopted a benevolent, paternalistic attitude toward the Indians clustered around its edge. Such a relationship is complex, for it involves many, often contradictory, emotions—sympathy, contempt, kindness, cruelty, mistrust, loyalty, generosity selfishness, altriusm, and apathy. None of these terms alone is capable of characterizing the situation that existed. Some mothers in Lovelock objected to Annie's presence at an otherwise all-white school and forbade their children to play with her. But again, it was a white storekeeper who, indignant at Lowry's desertion of his wife and child, gave them food and clothing without any guarantee that he would be repaid. Annie's experiences dramatize the general Indian-white relationship. It is seen that the white community was usually sympathetic to the Indians. Doctors willingly tended their sick and injured, and the townspeople lent them tools so that they could more easily move the houses when deaths did occur. And certainly the local citizens were not responsible for the short-sighted federal policy which affected all the Indians in America. Nevertheless, paternalism served to hide the tension that existed between the two cultures and to obscure the real needs of the Indians. Loyalties that did exist between individuals did not bridge the gap between the two races.

One of the more interesting figures described by Annie Lowry is that of the Paiute leader known as Cap John, whose Indian name, Samaranido, meant "patting raw meat."[120] Attempts to document or to supplement Annie Lowry's description of Cap John are generally inconclusive and often raise more questions than they answer, but we know that Cap John lived and that he was a man of some importance. If estimates of his age are reasonably accurate, he was born at a time when western Nevada was virtually untouched by civilization, perhaps even before the first trappers reached the Humboldt. Then, an accident of history, the discovery of gold in California and later in Nevada, turned the Humboldt into a highroad and the meadows into pasture land, dealing a death blow to life as he had known it. Cap John, as a leader, faced problems that his fathers had never known, for he had to contend with a culture that was numerically and technologically superior to his own, a culture that herded the Indians about like ill-tended cattle, ignorant of their needs and deaf to their protests. Unable to forcibly resist the new civilization and unable to find a place within it, Cap John's position was not an easy one; that much we can infer. But he is not portrayed as faultless and we do not rediscover in Cap John the Noble Savage. While he and his race were undoubtedly abused, he seems to have shared the faults common to all men—some measure of avarice and jealousy, perhaps brutality and cruelty as well. However, the position he maintained among the Paiutes indicates that he also commanded their respect.

Of Annie and Susie we have more known facts, although it is impossible to say exactly when Susie was born. If the chronology of the story is to be trusted, the date must have been before 1850, perhaps as early as 1836. Annie, herself, she believed, was born in 1867.[121] She died April 20, 1943.

She was, like Cap John, a product of the curious relationship between the two cultures, for she was, quite literally, the child of both. Though she was half white, and spent her childhood in the schools of white children, she could be quite Indian when it suited her. Mrs. Scott was told that when the local school teacher attempted to tell Annie of her grandchild's misbehavior, Annie would only sit and shake her head, indicating that she was unable to understand, although she spoke English fluently and everyone in Lovelock knew it. Yet the situation which fostered this humorous bit of perversity enabled her to tell a story which is a rarity, a tale told from the unique position of the half-breed and valuable for that reason if for no other. Generally, her objectivity would seem remarkable. This is not to say that she is without prejudices, but rather that her prejudices are well distributed, for she praises and condemns both races equally. In her descriptions of Indian beliefs, she sometimes betrays European concepts. When telling of the Indian religion, for instance, she frequently made mention of a figure known as the Big Man, a monotheistic deity that was unknown to the Paiutes before the coming of Christianity. At the same time, she firmly believed in the power of the Indian doctors. When her children became ill, she was as likely to take them to the Indian doctor as to the white. Thus, even when Annie Lowry's descriptions of aboriginal culture are at fault, she presents in herself a picture of her generation, in transition between two worlds. The anthropologists have recorded comparatively little. This narrative tells in understandable language a story as seen from the Indian point of view.

NOTES

¹ The corrosive effect of the white man upon the Indian seems to have been one of Annie's favorite themes. In 1909 she told Miss Mabel L. Reed, a senior at the University of Nevada, that "The white man through his whiskey and other influences has brought to the Indians degr[ad]ation and sorrow and has left them to fight out their lives without the superior knowledge and civilization of the white man." "History of the Development of Lovelock Valley" (unpublished B.A. thesis, University of Nevada, 1909), p. 21. The thesis has been most useful in checking the authenticity of this work, for it contains several parallel accounts as told by Annie and other Indians of Lovelock some twenty-seven years prior to the present account.

² Annie's opinion of the moral standards of the younger generation seems to represent that of most of the older Indians. Omer C. Stewart, "Northern Paiute Bands," *Anthropological Records,* II, No. 3 (1939), 442.

³ The Paiute women consider the term "squaw" pejorative and resent its use. During her conversations with the author, Annie Lowry used it only to express the attitude of the whites toward Indian women.

⁴ Annie was quite positive about this, but several modern commentators find themselves in disagreement on the point. Frank G. Roe, in *The Indian and the Horse* (Norman: University of Oklahoma Press, 1955), p. 79, states that the Paiutes owned horses by 1700 at the latest. However, editors John C. Ewers (see Leonard, *Adventures of Zenas Leonard, Fur Trader* [Norman: University of Oklahoma Press, 1959], p. 49, n. 28) and William H. Ellison (see Nidever, *The Life and Adventures of George Nidever* [Berkeley: University of California Press, 1939], p. 103, n. 74) say that the Paiutes did *not* have horses. The question is partially answered by referring to Ogden, who found horse tracks on the banks of the Humboldt and who mentions that one of his trappers was pursued by mounted Indians when his party was camped at the Sink in

1829. "The Peter Skene Ogden Journals; Snake Country Expedition, 1827–28 and 1828–29," ed. T. C. Elliott, *Oregon Historical Society Quarterly,* II (December, 1910), 393–395, hereafter referred to as "Ogden Journals." The Paiutes probably did not own many horses, but the Humboldt bands must have been acquainted with them by the time the first white men came.

⁵ Sarah Winnemucca describes the early emigrants in similar terms: "They had hair on their faces, and had white eyes, and looked beautiful," meaning that they had beards and blue eyes. The white men, with only their eyes and noses peeping through this foliage, reminded the Indians of owls, birds of bad omen, and they were often described as such by the Paiutes. See Sarah Winnemucca Hopkins, *Life Among the Paiutes; Their Wrongs and Claims,* ed. Mrs. Horace Mann (Boston: Putnam's, 1883), pp. 20, 25.

⁶ The yattah (or yata) is a Northern Paiute hulling basket, coarsely woven of willow in the shape of a flat, triangular tray. As indicated here, it was used for the hulling and winnowing of large seeds such as pinenuts.

⁷ Humboldt Lake is the lower terminus of the Humboldt River. The lake is commonly, and more appropriately, called the Humboldt Sink, for its bed is dry for a good part of the year. During the spring its brackish waters made the lake a popular camping place for the Indians.

⁸ Nick Jackson, a Reno collector of Indian lore and artifacts, suggests that the story of the "otter men" is a corruption of an Indian legend, which has it that the eagle felt sorry for a family of woodchucks who could not cross a stream. The eagle promised that if they would worship him, they would be given the power to swim. The mother agreed and was changed into a muskrat. The brother agreed and became a beaver. The father agreed and became an otter. However, the sister would not agree, for she was proud, and remained a woodchuck. As punishment, she alone was completely worthless and had but a poor coat of fur to keep her warm. Over the years, people took the eagle feathers and put them behind their ears to give them the power of the otter, the muskrat, and the beaver.

⁹ The area known as the Big Meadows, just above the Humboldt Sink, was later to become well known to the emigrants as the last fertile area on the river. The Granite Point mentioned here is a large granite outcropping located appproximately seven miles southwest of modern Lovelock. It soon became a landmark of the Humboldt

Trail and later became the site of one of the earliest trading stations in the area.

¹⁰ The common tule, a bulrush (*scirpus*) growing from three to nine feet in height, was found in profusion in the marshy areas of the Great Basin. The Indians not only ate the roots, but used the stalks to thatch their huts and in the building of small rafts.

¹¹ The karnee was one of several types of shelter built by the Northern Paiutes. A typical karnee was dome-shaped, and consisted of a light wooden framework covered with sagebrush, grass, or tule mats. A more detailed description follows in Chapter 13.

¹² The Forty Mile Desert was one of the most difficult and dangerous portions of the Overland Trail to California, the scene of terrible suffering and death to both livestock and emigrants. It is an alkaline waste forming the bed of old Lake Lahontan, and lies roughly south of Humboldt Sink, extending westerly to the Truckee River at Wadsworth, and southerly to the Carson River at old Ragtown, east of Fallon.

¹³ Appropriately named, Ragged Top Mountain is located about eighteen miles southwest of Lovelock. The south end of Pyramid Lake lies approximately thirty-eight miles directly beyond.

¹⁴ The Indian name for the Stillwater Range, located east of Carson Sink. It should not be confused with the Pine Nut Mountains of California.

¹⁵ This appears to be the mountain of that name within the Stillwater Range rather than the peak fifty miles northeast of Lovelock.

¹⁶ See Hopkins, pp. 11–12. In this account Sarah Winnemucca and her cousin, a little girl, were buried. She makes no mention of Muddlebury Canyon (also spelled Muddleberry, Muttleberry), but it would provide a natural route into the Humboldt Range. When questioned about hiding children in this way, Nick Jackson's informants thought the idea ridiculous, for the children would be left to the mercy of heat, cold, and wild animals, and would be likely to smother. In time of danger, the Indians' first concern was for the safety of their women and children.

¹⁷ Bighorn sheep, deer, and antelope were all found in the region, but there is no evidence that they were ever a major source of food for the Indians. Rabbits and ground squirrels were the Paiutes' main source of meat, and the white men never seriously competed for such fare. However, there is evidence that they did use the beaver for food and clothing to some extent. In 1828 Ogden complained that the Indians on the Humboldt wore moccasins of beaver hide and had made the animals wild by their hunt-

ing. ("Ogden Journals," p. 385.) Much later, O. C. Stewart was told that beaver were sometimes eaten. ("Northern Paiute," p. 372.) Nevertheless, there is no reason to believe that the beaver was as important to the Indians as Annie Lowry implies.

[18] Peter Skene Ogden, the able commander of the Snake River Brigade of the Hudson's Bay Company from 1824 to 1830, discovered the Humboldt River on November 9, 1828, and his band immediately began to strip the area of its furs. After moving eastward along its banks for a month, the party ran short of food and was forced by hunger to the more hospitable region of northern Utah.

[19] One of Ogden's men, Joseph Paul, became too ill to travel and was left with two companions in what was once thought to be the vicinity of what was later to become Mill City. On his return from Utah the following April, Ogden was met by his two men who told him that Paul had died and been buried where they camped. The party then followed the river to the Sink, were turned back by a band of semi-hostile Indians, and returned to the company's main quarters at Fort Vancouver.

[20] The mention of the Indians gathering at Paul's grave is given here substantially as Annie Lowry told it to the author, but there are reasons to suspect that the account is not entirely genuine. Upon reading this portion of the manuscript, Margaret Wheat, known for her special understanding of Nevada ethnology, pointed out that it would be most unlike the Indians to choose a grave for their meeting place. The Paiutes were quite wary of the spirits of the dead and were careful not to disturb them. Furthermore, historians no longer believe, as they once did, that Paul was buried at Mill City. This idea seems to have been based on the incomplete Laut transcriptions of Ogden's Journals, edited by T. C. Elliott and printed in the *Oregon Historical Society Quarterly* in 1910, and for many years the only available version of them. On the basis of more complete material, historians have revised their earlier ideas. Gloria G. Cline believes that Paul died in the vicinity of Carlin, Nevada, and is confirmed in this by Ogden's map, which shows the approximate location of the grave. (See Gloria Griffen Cline, *Exploring the Great Basin,* [Norman: University of Oklahoma Press, 1963], p. 122 and map following p. 46.) While it is not improbable that the Indians held a rendezvous at the site of Mill City, Annie Lowry seems to be responsible for adding the detail about Joseph Paul.

[21] Some of the older Indians of Lovelock used to tell of their first

encounter with the white men in the Humboldt Valley. When Annie Lowry repeated the story, she assumed that this meeting was Joseph Walker's "Battle of the Lakes," and spoke of it in those terms. Details of the battle were taken from a published account written by Zenas Leonard, one of Walker's men. See Leonard, pp. 69–72.

[22] A less elaborate description of the Paiutes' first meeting with the white man survives in the Reed manuscript, pp. 17–19. According to Mr. John O'Kane, who was told the story of Cap John and others, the Indians of Lovelock Valley had heard of the white men but had never seen any until a party of them appeared in the vicinity of Oreana. The valley was at that time mostly under water, and the white men rode along the sand hills on the west side of the river until they camped in a grove of cottonwoods and willows. The Indians were curious to see what the intruders looked like and crept closer. Seeing a large number of Indians, all of them carrying bows and arrows, the white men became excited and fired into the group, killing a number of them.

Although the Indians had had no intention of attacking the camp, they were angered by the treatment they received and sent to neighboring bands for reinforcements. On the following morning they surrounded the camp and closed in, only to find that the white men had buried their baggage during the night and had slipped away. The Indians dug up what was buried and had a celebration, but they never forgot their first meeting with the white race.

The account given by Reed seems to be a fair representation of the story as it was originally told by the Indians, but still the white party cannot be identified with any degree of certainty. The general circumstances of the clash seem to be those described by Leonard, Ewers, op. cit.; Washington Irving, The Adventures of Captain Bonneville, U.S.A., in the Rocky Mountains and the Far West (New York: G. P. Putnam's, 1868), pp. 407–408, hereafter cited as Irving; and Nidever, Ellison, op. cit., pp. 32–33, but none of these mentions the loss of their baggage or the escape by night.

[23] A Captain John is mentioned as a relative of Captain Truckee, who aided a white party in 1844. It is probable that he was the Cap John who, during the Indian wars of 1865, agreed to lead his followers out of a troubled area rather than join hostilities against white settlers, and it may be that he, like others, actually cooperated in the extermination of the less peaceful bands of his own people (Humboldt Register, April 22, 1865). If so, his actions are open to some interpretation; by his neutrality or his active coopera-

tion, he undoubtedly saved his own followers from disaster, but those not of his party suspected him of mere opportunism and treachery. It should not be thought, however, that he was a passive tool of the white, although belligerence on his part would have been foolish, leading only to defeat. But Cap John was not always silent. Letters in the National Archives indicate that Cap John was vocal in his protests against the treatment of his people, asking for the aid so often promised but so seldom received.

His name appears in a bewildering variety of sources—newspapers, letters, histories, personal recollections, census records—published and unpublished. Similarities of time, place, and circumstances lead one to suspect that they refer to the same figure that Annie describes. Temptation to accept Annie's composite picture of him is strong, but such an uncritical reconstruction of Cap John's life and character would be unwarranted, ignoring several inconsistencies and discrepancies.

[24] The older residents of Lovelock were familiar with the story that Cap John had once met Frémont and acted as guide for the explorer, who rewarded him with a letter and an American flag. (Cap John's flag is mentioned elsewhere, though Frémont is not mentioned in connection with it. See Chapter 10 and note 70.) As the evidence was buried with Cap John, it is now impossible to determine the authenticity of the story. It is neither impossible nor improbable that the two met, and Frémont often gave gifts to those Indians he encountered, but his journals do not bear out the story as it is told here, and, as the notes indicate, several points of the story are subject to challenge. In any case, the circumstances were probably different from those described above. Several of the details concerning Frémont's expeditions are obviously drawn from published sources.

[25] Frémont, who was still a lieutenant at the time of the second expedition, left a detailed description of his visit to Pyramid Lake, which he and Kit Carson discovered on January 10, 1844. He described the "salmon trout" (not "salmon and trout"), but none of the Indians he met there resembles Cap John. All communication was carried on by signs, and Frémont was able to learn of the surrounding area only by means of maps drawn for him on the ground. Had he met an English-speaking Indian here he would hardly have failed to mention it. But when he asked for a guide, he received only self-conscious laughter and he was forced to find his own way to Walker Lake. See John C. Frémont, *Report of the Exploring Expedition to the Rocky Mountains in the year 1842, and*

to Oregon and North California in the Years 1843-44, 28 Cong., 2 Sess., House Exec. Doc. 166 (1845), pp. 219-221.

26 The account confuses the circumstances of two of Frémont's expeditions. Walker did not accompany the second, in 1843-44, but the third, which began in 1845. It was on this expedition that Frémont divided his party upon reaching the Humboldt, sending one party down the river with Walker while he himself cut to the southwest through the central portion of what is now Nevada. Since neither Frémont nor Walker visited Pyramid Lake on the third expedition, Cap John could not have met them under the circumstances described above.

27 According to a widely accepted story, Truckee, leader of a Humboldt band, and several young Indians accompanied Frémont to California on his third expedition. One of these Indians, named "Captain Juan," described by William Wright (Dan de Quille), resembles Cap John in many respects. However, there is no agreement among authorities. In an unpublished paper now being prepared, entitled "Frémont and Captain Truckee: Historians as Myth Makers," Dr. Willard Z. Park contends that no Nevada Indians crossed into California with Frémont. Certainly Frémont himself makes no mention of these Indians in his detailed journals, and held most of the Basin Indians in contempt, only a step removed from animal creation. The earliest published reference to the story of Truckee and Frémont, says Dr. Park, seems to be that in Wright's *Washoe Rambles*, first published in 1861, and the story has been repeated by historians and anthropologists (and now by Annie Lowry) until "myth has become sanctified as history." In the absence of corroborating evidence it should be received with some skepticism. See William Wright, *The Big Bonanza,* (New York: A. A. Knopf, 1959), pp. 204-205; Hopkins, pp. 8-10; and Robert F. Heizer, *Notes on Some Paviotso Personalities and Material Culture,* ("Nevada State Museum Anthropological Papers," No. 2 [Carson City: January, 1960]), 1, n. 1, hereafter referred to as Heizer, "Notes."

28 Carpenter's Ranch was located approximately one and one-half miles south of Lovelock near the site of the present Circle-L Ranch.

29 It is improbable that Cap John's commercial ventures began before the mid-fifties. Significant numbers of emigrants did not begin to come over the Humboldt Trail until 1845, and as late as 1849 Vincent Geiger and Wakeman Bryarly had little trouble in cutting enough grass for their own animals even though two

hundred wagons had reached the Meadows before them. See Vincent Geiger and Wakeman Bryarly, *Trail to California*, (New Haven: Yale University Press, 1945), pp. 182–186. Even after this time the operation of a trading station would have been only a seasonal business. Wagon trains began arriving in the area in mid-July and continued to pass through until mid-September. The Reed manuscript (p. 26) states that there was no farming in the Lovelock area until the railroad came through (1868), and that the few permanent inhabitants cut hay for sale to the emigrants. Cap John probably traded during these months and supplemented his income by various means during the rest of the year. But by 1862, the population had become more stable and the season began earlier. In a letter dated May 1, 1862, John A. Burche, Local Agent, Humboldt District, wrote J. Y. Lockhart, Superintendent, Carson City, telling of the deplorable condition of the Indians during February, adding "in the Humboldt, Big Meadows . . . they have built two or three willow houses as they commenced the business of ranching, cutting hay and selling to the emigrants." (National Archives, Record Group 75, Nevada Superintendency.) The emigrants here referred to are probably miners from the California and Comstock mines moving to the new strikes near what is now Lovelock, Nevada.

[30] Reportedly, Cap John continued to "read" Frémont's letter from memory even after he became completely blind in his old age. Although Cap John's experiences with Frémont may not have been as they are described in the text, the value placed upon such a letter would have been characteristic. Randolph B. Marcy, in *The Prairie Traveler* (New York: Harper & brothers, 1859), remarked that the Indians ". . . are always desirous of procuring, from whomsoever they meet, testimonials of their good behavior, which they preserve with great care, and exhibit upon all occasions to strangers as a guarantee of future good conduct." (Wright, in *The Big Bonanza*, pp. 200–201, says that Captain Truckee was buried with Frémont's letter folded in his left hand.) At Pyramid Lake in 1903, Dr. C. Hart Merriam photographed an old Indian who still wore a medal given to him by Frémont over half a century before. Heizer, "Notes," pp. 5, 13.

[31] Polygamy was practiced by some Paiutes, though it was not as common in aboriginal times as Annie implies. In this respect, as in others, Cap John seems to have fared well. In 1880, Cap John, age 50, was the husband of two wives and the father of five children. No occupation is listed in the 1880 census for Cap John, but both

Nettie and Magie [sic], age 40 and 30 respectively, were washer-women. *United States Census, 1880,* p. 14.

[32] It should be remembered that Cap John's affluence should be measured in terms of the Indians' values, if indeed his situation differed greatly from theirs. In 1870, J. P. Hamilton, superintendent of the Central Pacific Railroad, wrote a letter to the superintendent of the Nevada Agency in Carson City on behalf of "Captain John, Chief of the Paiutes on the Humboldt River," complaining of the extreme poverty of his people and asking assistance to prevent their starvation. (National Archives, Record Group 75, Nevada Superintendency.) It would seem that Cap John should be remembered not as much for his reputed prosperity as for his position as a leader and spokesman on behalf of his followers.

[33] Old Winnemucca was the most influential leader of the Paiutes during the Indian Wars of the 1860's. He was succeeded by his son, Natchez. The causes of the tribal division are more fully treated in a following chapter.

[34] Primitive people commonly stand in awe and fear of the woman's menstrual blood, and the Paiutes were no exception. The shaman (medicine man) cured his tobacco in a secret place lest a woman in this condition should touch it or come near it and endanger his healing powers. Menstruating women were excluded from antelope drives in the belief that the animals would break through the circle at the point where the woman stood. (Willard Z. Park, *Shamanism in Western North America,* "Publications in Social Sciences," No. 2 [Evanston, Ill.: Northwestern University, 1938], pp. 35, 65). The Indians knew only that the woman was being visited by some mysterious power which was as likely as not to be harmful, and it was thought better for all concerned that she be kept in some degree of isolation.

Customs differed among the different Paiute bands, and the Indians of the Lovelock area seem to have been particularly strict. The woman was banished to a hut at the edge of camp for five days. While she was there she abstained from eating certain foods, such as meat, grease, and salt, and she was forbidden to touch her head with her hands. (An intolerable itch could be scratched with a stick if necessary.) After she was cleansed, the woman bathed, dressed in new clothing, painted herself, and returned to camp as described above. (See Stewart, "Northern Paiute," p. 411.) However, Annie, who was one of Stewart's informants, had earlier told Robert H. Lowie that even in her mother's time the seclusion of women was a Shoshone custom, not Paiute. *Notes on Shoshonean*

Ethnography, "American Museum of Natural History Anthropological Papers," XX (1924), 273; Hopkins, p. 48.

[35] It was particularly important that the groom be satisfactory to the bride's parents, for the young couple usually lived with them (though not always) and contributed to their support until the new family was large enough to warrant a separate establishment. But it is not so certain that the bride had no voice in the matter. Sarah Winnemucca (Hopkins, p. 49) said that the bride was never forced to marry against her wishes, and Park says that the girl had the option of moving her bed if she did not wish the marriage to be consummated. Willard Z. Park, "Paviotso Polyandry," *American Anthropologist*, XXXIX (1937), 367.

[36] Annie was quite insistent on this point, for she also told Omer Stewart that women were stoned for deserting their husbands ("Northern Paiute," p. 439). And the opinion seems to have had some currency among the white people at the time. (See, for instance, Thomas Wren, *A History of the State of Nevada* [New York: Lewis Publishing Company, 1904], p. 310.) But this does not seem to have been the general opinion among the Indians themselves. Stewart's other informants generally agreed that there were legitimate grounds for divorce ("Northern Paiute," p. 405), but it seems to have been uncommon (Park, "Paviotso Polyandry," p. 367). There was, of course, the possibility that an enraged husband or his family might beat or kill an erring wife, but this was a personal affair and did not involve the band (Lowie, "Shoshonean Ethnography," p. 227). (See also Robert F. Heizer, *Executions by Stoning Among the Sierra Miwok and Northern Paiute*, "Kroeber Anthropological Society Papers," No. 12, Berkeley: University of California, 1955.) It may be that Annie's opinion was influenced by the fact that her own mother was twice deserted.

[37] Animal skins of any size were scarce in the more barren areas of the Great Basin. Early Paiute women wore only a skirt of grass or pounded sagebrush bark during the summer and the men wore even less. Later, Paiutes of both sexes wore more clothing, possibly because the horse and rifle made deerskin more easy to obtain.

[38] The Shoshones evidently mistook the bright red cinnabar for harmless iron ore. Cinnabar is, of course, the ore from which mercury is obtained, and the Indians died from mercury poisoning.

[39] "Wee-pah" is possibly a shortened form of "wipanabu," the Paiute name for "Big Milkweed" (*Asclepias speciosa*), one of several plants used in making cord and twine.

40 The phrase "chief of all the Paiutes" is misleading. The Paiute people lived in a number of autonomous bands, each led by an individual whose authority derived from the respect accorded him by his followers. However, the increasing tensions caused by white emigrants and the Indian wars of the sixties probably helped to centralize the authority of several "chiefs" in western Nevada, the most famous of which was Old Winnemucca. (See Heizer, "Notes," Appendix, p. 6.) The band living in the Lovelock area is identified by Stewart as the Kupa-dokado, and by Park as the Hapud-tukede. The names are probably allomorphic forms meaning "ground-squirrel eaters" (*kupa* being the Paiute word for ground-squirrel, -*dokado* a suffix meaning "eaters"). See Omer Stewart, "Northern Paiute," p. 363; and Willard Z. Park, *et al.*, "Tribal Distribution in the Great Basin," *American Anthropologist*, XL, No. 4 (1938), 622.

41 The Big Man is more fully discussed in note 52.

42 The facts seem to be confused for it is geographically impossible to go "all the way be water" from either Pyramid Lake or Reno to the Humboldt Sink. Indians living on the Carson River could easily cross the Carson Sink to Humboldt Sink, but the Pyramid Lake bands and those living in the Reno area would have taken the route over the Nightingale Range and past Ragged Top Mountain. Old Truckee, who is remembered as a friend to the early emigrants and to Frémont, was a leader of the band living on the lower Humboldt. Heizer, "Notes," p. 1, n. 1.

43 For the aboriginal Paiute, life was one continuous search for food. At certain seasons some of the animals could be more efficiently hunted in communal drives, and the description of the mudhen hunt is representative of one type.

44 These boats, or "balsas," were capable of carrying only one man and a small quantity of goods or game. Normally they were poled through the shallow waters of the lakes, not paddled, or else the hunter waded and pulled or pushed the loaded raft along. Margaret M. Wheat describes the construction of such a boat in her illustrated *Notes on Paviotso Material Culture*, "Nevada State Museum Anthropological Papers," No. 1 (Carson City: October, 1959), pp. 5–6.

45There is some basis for the description of Mo-be-ti-wak. His reputation for strength would seem to be borne out by the story of his death. The author was told that Mo-be-ti-wak was murdered by members of his own tribe, perhaps near Pyramid Lake. It is said that after a violent struggle he was overcome and decapitated, but that the headless body continued to thrash about for some time afterwards. However, there are indications that the name "Mo-be-ti-wak," the description given in the text, and the anecdote have been confused. In 1931, Heizer ("Notes," p. 2) was told by an informant that "Mubetewaka" was the Indian name of the chief known to the whites as "Old Winnemucca." The name "Mubetewaka," which was said to mean "man with hole in his nose," would seem appropriate, for contemporary photographs of Winnemucca depict a dignified old man with a bone thrust through the septum of his nose. (See, for instance, the illustration in Myron Angel's *History of Nevada*, a reproduction of Thompson and West's edition of 1881 [Berkeley: Howell-North Books, 1958] facing p. 144.)

[46] In Sarah Winnemucca's account, her grandfather, Old Truckee, was presented with a tin plate which delighted him so much that he summoned his band together to show it off. He bored holes in the plate and wore it for some time as a headdress until, in California with Frémont, he was told of its real purpose. Truckee bore the jokes of his "white brothers" with good humor. Hopkins, pp. 7, 26.

[47] White Cloud City was situated east of Carson Sink in the Stillwater Range. Like so many of the mining towns of the last century, it has disappeared.

[48] The story of the epidemic is a composite account drawn from several sources. Annie Lowry knew of such an epidemic. Her description, as told by Mabel Reed in 1909, is as follows:

"The Paiutes of Big Meadows were once almost exterminated by cholera. After becoming firmly established and prospering in Lovelock Valley the tribe numbered between eight and nine hundred. The plague when it disappeared left something like eighty people. The Indians tell of how the people stricken by the dread disease tried to cross the mountains, thinking they could get away from it, but as a result all these perished and dead bodies were strewn for miles around through the surrounding hills. From the remnant of Indians left was built the Paiute tribe which existed at the time the white man appeared." Reed, "Lovelock Valley," p. 17.

Note that in the Reed account the estimate of the size of the tribe is much smaller than that given in this text, and that the incident took place before the coming of the white man. But the mortality rate of approximately 90 percent (which seems to be greatly exaggerated) is the same in both.

The details of the author's description originated with one Natchez who told the story to Captain Dave. Dave in turn told his son,

Bo-we-an (Skinny Dave), who related the story to John T. Reid. It was Natchez who saw the dead mother with the child crawling over her and it was he who blamed the sickness on the white emigrants who wanted the Indians' land. Historically, it is probable that the disease was unwittingly transmitted to the Indians by the California emigrants who suffered from the disease in 1849 and for several years thereafter. Although the epidemic had abated by the time their wagon trains reached the Basin area, the contaminated waters of the Humboldt and the flies that swarmed on the hundreds of dead cattle that lay beside it would be sufficient to carry the bacillus to the unimmunized Indians along its banks. But in no case would the disease have affected the wildlife as described above. See also Hopkins, p. 41.

[49] The reference is clearly to Lovelock Cave, the archaeology of which is described by L. L. Loud and M. R. Harrington, *Lovelock Cave*, "Publications in American Archaeology and Ethnology," XXV, No. 1 (Berkeley: University of California Press, 1929).

[50] According to Margaret Wheat, storytelling was the Paiutes' favorite diversion during the long winter evenings. Custom dictated that once a story was begun, it had to be finished, even though everyone but the narrator had fallen asleep.

[51] This rule seems to have been relaxed to some degree in later days. During the 1930's one well-known shaman at Pyramid Lake specialized in cases of difficult labor. Whether or not he assisted in actual delivery was not mentioned. Park, *Shamanism*, p. 47.

[52] There is no Paiute spirit or deity known as the Big Man. In his aboriginal state the Indian recognized not one, but a number of powerful spirits which regulated his everyday life. However, the reference to the Big Man's footprints suggests some relationship with a mythical figure who appears in several Indian tales recorded by Robert H. Lowie ("Shoshonean Tales," *Journal of American Folklore*, XXXVII, Nos. 143–144, 1924, p. 208). This figure, known as "The Man" or "The Old Man," corresponds to the Judeo-Christian creator in that he formed a number of local geographical figures. At the same time he corresponds to Adam insofar as he and his wife were the parents of the Paiute People. According to tradition, The Man left his footprints in several places where they were seen by the Indians. But The Man seems to have been a passive, historical figure, having little or nothing to do with the conduct of the Indians' everyday life. It would seem then that the Big Man of this text is a fusion in Annie's mind of the mythical figure and the monotheistic Christian God. It may be, as was suggested

by Mrs. Nellie Basso of Lovelock, that the Big Man's footprints were in reality those left by the giant ground sloth that once roamed western Nevada.

[53] That is, before the schism between the followers of Cap John and those of Winnemucca, mentioned in Chapter 5.

[54] Aside from a number of depradations and murders committed by individuals or small bands, the Paiutes made no concerted efforts to drive out the white men before the Indian War of 1860, twenty years or more after major trapping expeditions had ceased to travel along the Humboldt.

[55] Historically, Natchez was the son of Old Winnemucca, not his cousin, but Annie Lowry denied this. Annie told the author that Old Winnemucca was the father of Lee, Marie, and Suzie, and that Natchez, Tom, and Sarah Winnemucca were cousins of these three. There seems to be no evidence to confirm this opinion. Dr. Park, who attempted to get an accurate account of the entire Winnemucca family in 1933 and 1934, thinks the task is now impossible. Even at that time he could not obtain accurate statements, partly because the Winnemucca name has become a status symbol (at least in relation to the whites) and informants are often eager to claim it if there is a chance of being believed.

[56] On the basis of the account given here it is impossible to locate this particular incident historically, or even to verify it. (In some ways it is similar to a battle described in Angel's *History*, p. 170, and Hopkins, p. 77, but even these accounts are to some degree contradictory.) The Indian wars of the 1860's were nothing more than a series of bloody raids and counter-raids by Indians and whites alike, and one side had no more claim to honor than the other. In many instances the soldiers were guided or actively aided by Paiutes, some of whom believed that the survival of their people lay in cooperation with the whites, and others who hoped for personal gain. Understandably the wars left the Paiute people divided into a number of hostile factions. Even in 1936 the Lovelock Indian Colony was divided into at least two distinct groups, and anyone who became associated with one faction found himself rigidly excluded from the other.

[57] More time had elapsed between these two occasions than is implied here. The Battle of Pyramid Lake took place May 11, 1860, and the Central Pacific Railroad was laid through "Lovelock's" in 1868.

[58] The Chinese laborers, who themselves had little enough to eat, were probably not motivated by simple generosity. David Myrick, in *Railroads of Nevada and Eastern California*, I (Berkeley, Calif.:

Howell-North Books, 1962) p. 18, says that the Central Pacific grading crews were often the victims of the lazier and less scrupulous Indians, who soon discovered that after being sufficiently harassed and terrorized the Chinese were willing to buy peace with food.

[59] The Shoshones were simply following a practice established long before the coming of the white men. The Paiutes, Washoes, and Shoshones observed no strict political boundaries, but each claimed its respective food-gathering area. Occasionally one tribe, in full knowledge that they were trespassing, would invade its neighbor's territory in search of food and would continue to do so until the invasion ended in a clash. The losers, of course, retreated to a nondisputed area. As the railroad moved eastward into the land of the Shoshones (which began in the general vicinity of Golconda), the inhabitants asserted their claim to the white men's garbage, just as they had formerly claimed the natural food in the area, and drove the Paiutes away. (See Willard Z. Park, *et al.*, "Tribal Distribution in the Great Basin," pp. 623–624.)

[60] "Malapai" is not slag, but any type of rock formed under great heat and pressure. Such rock never bears precious metals and is to the prospector "evil rock."

[61] The author was told a similar story by Bo-we-an (Skinny Dave), policeman of the Lovelock Indian Colony. "There is a legend among the Paiutes that one time the earth shook so nobody could stand up. The Indians all were thrown to the ground for half an hour. They had to hold on to sagebrush to keep from being tumbled in all directions. The earth shook violently as it never had before and never has since."

[62] This is reference to the Battle of Pyramid Lake, May 11, 1860. Knowing that they would be attacked in retaliation for the killing of several men at William's Station (an incident which does not seem to have been unprovoked), the Paiutes massed their forces and killed nearly half of the undisciplined volunteers sent against them. See Angel's *History*, pp. 152 ff.; Hubert H. Bancroft, *History of Nevada, Colorado, and Wyoming, 1540–1888* (San Francisco: The History Co., 1890), pp. 209 ff.

[63] Warren Wasson seems to have been one of the few conscientious Indian agents to serve in western Nevada. By one account Wasson had just finished dividing a ration of clothing to the band at Pyramid Lake when an old man arrived, too late to receive a share. Seeing that he was much disapppointed, Wasson stripped off his own shirt and drawers and presented them to the latecomer. Although he served for only two years (1860–1862), his courage

and generosity left a lasting impression upon the Indians. (Angel, *History*, p. 165.) Annie Lowry's eldest daughter, Eva, was once married to an Indian who is said to have been named after Wasson.

[64] The smelter, which was built ca. 1868 to reduce the ore from the rich Montezuma mine, was claimed to be the first precious metal smelter in the United States. It was destroyed by fire in the late 1870's.

[65] Angel's *History* (p. 453) gives the superintendent's name as A. W. Nason.

[66] Old Oreana (as distinct from the modern village of that name) was situated on the banks of the Humboldt River, which supplied water for the smelter. The name was also adopted by the station on the Central Pacific Railroad, which eventually became the "Esspee," or Southern Pacific. The town was at one time larger than either Lovelock or Winnemucca and sported its share of stores, saloons, and brothels, but the population began to leave after the smelter burned and the ore veins ran out, and today nothing remains.

[67] The practice was perhaps not unknown, for Sarah Winnemucca charges her cousin, Captain Dave, with exposing his wife to the white men for money. (Hopkins, p. 98.) Yet Cap John's treatment of Sau-tau-nee and his wives does not accurately represent the normal relationship between the Paiute men and women. By most accounts the Paiute women were extremely virtuous. See, for example, William Wright's comments in *The Big Bonanza*, pp. 209–210: "The women are remarkable for their chastity, and are in this respect models not only for the women of all surrounding tribes, but for those of all nations and colors." Normally, Cap John's attempts to force Susie to marry him would arouse the indignation of his fellows and end with his ostracism.

[68] There are indications that this story is true. The Census of 1870 shows that Lowry, Louis N. Carpenter (not F. L. Carpenter as in the MS), and E. J. Brown all lived in Oreana. Lowry was then a stage driver, Carpenter a hotel-keeper, and Brown a quartz miner. Mrs. Hannah Wiley, one of the older residents of Lovelock, remembers Brown as "an old miner who was known for gambling around the country. He lost a lot of land to a man named Lowry." By 1880, the former stage driver had become a "farmer" employing seven men. In 1870, Carpenter—then only twenty-eight—claimed eight hundred dollars worth of property, and it may be that he staked Lowry in the poker game within a year or two after that

date. *United States Census, 1870* (Nevada, Humboldt County, Lake Township), p. 1; *United States Census, 1880* (Nevada, Humboldt County, Lake Township), p. 6.

[69] To "take the shawl" is to return to the Indian way of life.

[70] In 1900 Mabel Reed gave the following description of Cap John: "He died in Lovelock some ten years ago and was at that time between eighty and ninety years of age. . . . Captain John was to have been succeeded by his son now living at Pyramid Lake but the latter refused the honor saying that he could not talk like his father nor give such good advice. People now living in Lovelock tell of Capt. John's powerful voice and his great influence over his people. When he died he requested them to bury him wrapped in the American flag which he always draped back of him at the big fandangos when he spoke. The old Captain was totally blind years before his death." ("Lovelock Valley," pp. 19–20.) It should be remembered that Annie Lowry was one of Miss Reed's informants.

[71] Eva Pancho, Annie's oldest daughter, remembers the incident although she was only a small girl at the time. Cap John's son was known as Joe Lowry for he had worked for Jerome Lowry and had adopted his employer's name. He appears as a member of Lowry's household, as a laborer, in the 1880 census.

[72] The dispute caused by the beaver dam probably took place in 1880 or shortly thereafter. The census for that year shows that Mike McGovern was working for Lowry, and that Henry W. Fuss, a Prussian by birth, lived adjacent to Carpenter's Ranch. (His "household" of one is listed immediately after that of Lowry; logically the two were neighbors.) Annie, or "Anne," was seven at the time and would have been old enough to remember the incident.

[73] Although it is not impossible that Jerome Lowry knew Samuel Clemens at one time, Annie Lowry could hardly have seen him. Clemens came through Humboldt County on his initial journey to Carson City in the summer of 1861 and spent two months prospecting at Unionville during the following winter. His last visit to the state took place in 1868, before the establishment of Carpenter's Ranch and perhaps before Annie's birth. The mention of his visits to Jerome Lowry is possibly based on her childhood recollection of a photograph belonging to her father.

[74] Jerome Lowry was born in Maryland in 1840, but both of his parents were born in Virginia. *United States Census, 1880* (Humboldt County, Lake Township).

[75] The Blue Wing Range, appproximately twenty-five miles west of Lovelock.

[76] The name "Lowry Wells" survives on United States Geological Survey maps of the area. The well is located on the western slopes of the Trinity Range in the Velvet district. It lies on the natural trail to the Blue Wing Range.

[77] The story of the battle seems to have been well known to the older Indians around Lovelock. Sarah Winnemucca Hopkins (pp. 73–75) gives one account. Her version is reproduced with several others in the Loud and Harrington study, *Lovelock Cave*, pp. 162, 165–169. (Annie Lowry is mentioned as an informant by John T. Reid, p. 167.) See also O. C. Stewart, "Northern Paiute," pp. 440–441.

[78] The 1880 census lists the three sons of Louis Carpenter as William W., three years; Louis David ("Lumie" mistaken for Louis), two years; and Charles C., ten months. If Charlie was just learning to walk when Annie stayed at the Carpenters', the year was ca. 1882.

[79] Sarah Winnemucca Hopkins probably had this honor. During the 1880's she was entered in a school at San Jose, California, but the parents of the white children objected so much that she was forced to leave after three weeks. But she must have received more education than this, for she was writing her book at the appproximate time that Annie started school. (Hopkins, p. 70.)

[80] Cora Williams was four years older than Annie, and Maude was six years younger. As Maude was only one year old in 1880, the episode of the graveyard must have occurred about 1885, a few years later than Annie implies.

[81] The only Mrs. St. Clair in Lovelock at this time seems to have been Mrs. Robert St. Clair. Her concern for Jerome Lowry's domestic affairs may have been prompted by the fact that her husband was serving a twenty-five year sentence in the state prison for the murder of a neighbor. (Angel, *History*, p. 455.)

[82] Jackson Lowry was five years younger than Annie.

[83] Patrick and Anne Reid were the parents of five children, John T., Emmett, Paul, Agnes, and Francis. Both John and Paul contributed, indirectly, to this book.

[84] This type of rabbit brush (*Chrysothamnus nauseosus*) was known to the Indians as "sigup." The secretion was found at the top of the root. (O. C. Stewart, "Northern Paiute," p. 428.) The sap of milkweed, sego lilies, and pine trees was also used as gum.

[85] George Singer, a stonecutter, was not from Germany, but from France.

[86] John T. Reid, who accompanied the drive for one day's jour-

ney, told the author that Lowry settled in Jordan Valley in southeastern Oregon.

[87] Shinny is described in Chapter 15.

[88] It was at this time that the autographed picture of Mark Twain, mentioned earlier, was lost.

[89] E. D. Kelly became the editor of the *Silver State* in 1872 when the paper was published in Unionville. In 1874 the *Silver State* was moved to Winnemucca, and in 1875 Kelly became a partner to J. J. Hill and continued as editor.

[90] Sarah Winnemucca Hopkins confirms this in *Life Among the Paiutes*, p. 128.

[91] Possibly the wife of M. S. Bonnifield, Winnemucca attorney, with whom E. D. Kelly had been a partner in the *Humboldt Register* during 1869–1870. (Angel, *History*, p. 303.)

[92] A covered, round-bottomed, cast-iron skillet which stood on three legs. As the name implies, it could be used for either baking or frying.

[93] The year was ca. 1886, as Julia Sanny died February 28, 1934, at the age of 49. Julia's well-marked grave is located in the Indian cemetery at Lovelock.

[94] The white residents of Lovelock understood the significance of this custom. When the manager of the local power company asked an Indian why he wanted to borrow some tools, the Indian explained "Kid died," and he was given the equipment he asked for.

[95] See also the detailed, illustrated description of the construction of a cattail house given by Margaret M. Wheat in "Notes on Paviotso Material Culture," pp. 6–7.

[96] John T. Reid, who has been mentioned several times in both the text and notes, was born in Unionville in 1871 and was brought to Lovelock by his parents when he was still a small child. As a boy he worked in his father's store and at the age of twenty-five he became a mining engineer. Although he had only a public-school education, Mr. Reid was a man of unusually broad interests. He was a member of a number of scientific societies (including the Royal Society of London), and was co-author of a chapter of Sam P. Davis's *History of Nevada*. Reid also gained the friendship of the local Indians and learned much about their culture. Consequently he acted as a consultant to L. L. Loud and M. R. Harrington during their excavations of Lovelock Cave, and items from his large collection of Indian lore have found their way into several studies of the aboriginal culture of the area. The Reid collection is now in the possession of the Nevada Historical Society at Reno.

[97] As late as the end of the century there were still nineteen Indian doctors at Pyramid Lake in a community of seven hundred people. Park, *Shamanism*, p. 20.

[98] The chief function of the Indian doctor was the healing of disease, but it was thought that some doctors used their powers, not to heal, but to cause illness, misfortune, or death. Once the shaman had taken this course he felt a compulsion to kill one of his victims. If the doctor was particularly notorious, the band, rather than a family, might decide to rid themselves of the threat to their safety. For a more complete discussion of the sorcerer, see Park, *Shamanism*, pp. 43–45.

[99] Annie neglected to identify Sam.

[100] Like most aspects of Paiute culture, marriage customs fell into no strict pattern, and the details of courtship as described above did not necessarily obtain in all situations. In its simplest form, marriage was simply a matter of cohabitation; if a woman accepted a man sexually and the couple lived together, their marriage was recognized by the community without more formality. However, family ties among the Paiutes were normally very strong, and—assuming that the respective family units were intact—every effort would be made to insure the compatibility of the inlaws as well as that of the prospective couple. (In some cases this consideration might be of more importance than the feelings of the persons to be married.) Usually there was a preliminary discussion to determine the consent of the girl and her parents. The prospective groom then began to make nightly visits to the home of his intended where he sat quietly by the door, slept there that night, and left early the next morning. These visits might continue for days, weeks, or months until the girl's parents showed their approval by speaking pleasantly to the suitor and by offering him food. When the household had retired, the man lay down with his bride, and with the girl's consent, the marriage was consummated. To refuse, the girl needed only to get up and move her bed. (Park, "Paviotso Polyandry," p. 367.) Annie Lowry's description of Paiute courtship and marriage is similar to that given in Lowie's "Shoshonean Tales" (pp. 200, 207). After telling of the marriage of two mythical figures, Lowie's informant explained that the Indians used to be married in the same way: the man and woman never slept together on the first night, but gradually approached each other on successive nights for a week before intercourse.

[101] Annie's first child was born in 1889. If she herself was born in 1872 as the census records indicate, she could hardly have been

more than fifteen at the time of her marriage to Sanny. If, however, she was born in 1867, as she believed, she would have been more than twenty years old.

[102] Although the explanations given by Annie Lowry sound suspiciously like folk etymology, she seems to be at least partially correct. Lowie was told that girls were often named for flowers and that a child usually received a nickname which became permanent. ("Shoshonean Ethnography," p. 272.) There is, of course, no reason to assume that the specific examples given by Annie are valid. It is also said that Dot-so-la-lee's name is a corruption of the name of Doctor S. L. Lee, for whom she worked for many years. Unfortunately there seems to be no adequate study of the etymology of Paiute names. See also Hopkins, 46, n.

[103] For example, Cap John's son was known as Joe Lowry after Jerome (Joseph?) Lowry, his employer.

[104] The most interesting and puzzling archaeological discoveries of the area pertain not to the modern Paiute, but to an earlier culture. Artifacts are usually in an excellent state of preservation, due to the aridity of the atmosphere and soil, and radiocarbon tests have shown that some sites were occupied as early as 1218 B.C. A particular type of wicker—which has been named "Lovelock wicker"—is peculiar to this area, but neither the wicker nor a number of early implements are used or even recognized by living Indians. Consequently, the prehistoric cultures have not been definitely linked with the modern, and the connection can only be assumed. See Robert F. Heizer and Alex D. Krieger, *Archaeology of Humboldt Cave, Churchill County, Nevada*, "Publications in American Archaeology and Ethnology," Vol. XLVII, No. 1 (Berkeley: University of California Press, 1956), pp. 76, 87.

[105] Mrs. Springer's son.

[106] The graves of Jessie and his grandmother are well-marked. Jessie's headboard gives his date of death as October 14, 1903, and that of his grandmother, December 28, 1903.

[107] The material dealing with the smothering of those suffering with delirium did not originate with Annie. The author's notes state that Rosie, a Shoshone woman, told her employer, Mrs. Reed, that an old Indian had died and was talking with his grandmother, meaning that he was delirious. Although Rosie could speak little English, she was able to make her employer understand that unless the spirit was received in two days he would be helped into the next world. Later, Mrs. Reed was told by a doctor at Nixon that the practice was sometimes followed among the older Indians.

When questioned by the author, Annie denied knowing of such things. There seems to be no confirmation of this practice, and it is highly unlikely in view of the respect the Paiutes hold for their elders. Furthermore, the idea that people are punished after death to atone for sins committed on earth is completely foreign to Paiute beliefs.

[108] This game, known as "natzi'saka" by the Indians and as "shinny" by the anthropologist, was normally played only by the women. (O. C. Stewart, "Northern Paiute," p. 397.)

[109] The neatly kept Indian cemetery, located near the colony southwest of Lovelock, is still in use. The headboards standing over the graves of Annie's family have rounded tops terminating in "shoulders," and are painted as described above. Ironically, Annie's grave has no headboard.

[110] (Also kawono), a conical burden basket.

[111] Annie also told the story of the healing of her son to Lowie, who published a condensed account of it in "Shoshonean Ethnography" (p. 294). According to Lowie, Annie said that her son was placed, not next to the shaman, but face-down on top of him so that the pits of their stomachs were together. In other respects the two versions are similar.

[112] Despite its comparative simplicity and the minimum of public participation, the healing rite was virtually the only ceremonial activity practiced by the Paiutes. Some features, such as the feather wand, are fairly common, but the rite did not follow any strict pattern, and all of the descriptions given in the text may be taken as representative. For a thorough discussion of the Paviotso shamanistic complex, see W. Z. Park's *Shamanism*, pp. 1–71.

[113] John Pascal led an active and colorful life, but it is unlikely that he took part in an Indian campaign in 1876. The headboard of his grave at the Indian cemetery in Lovelock indicates that he died May 18, 1930, at the age of sixty-six years. If these figures are correct, Pascal was born in 1864 and was only twelve years old in 1876. Nevertheless, he did enjoy considerable fame in northern Nevada as a tracker. In January of 1911, he was called from Winnemucca to track the murderers of four ranchers killed near Little High Rock Canyon in the northwest corner of the state. After several days the pursuers caught an Indian band led by the renegade known as "Shoshone Mike" near Kelly Creek, north of Golconda, and the chase ended in a pitched battle. Thus Pascal helped to put down what seems to have been the last Indian uprising in the United States. (The Little High Rock incident is retold by Kenneth

D. Scott, in *Frozen Grass*, New York: Carlton Press, 1960.)
[114] The idea that the Big Man is the source of shamanistic power seems to be personal. The doctor's healing power is usually attributed to one or more of the spirits associated with animals, certain mountains and rocks, ghosts of the dead, water-babies, and water-serpents. See Park, *Shamanism*, pp. 15–20.

[115] The series of interviews which forms the basis of the narrative ended with the summer of 1936. Although the author and Annie met several times in the following years, their visits were entirely social. Annie Lowry died April 20, 1943.

[116] The following account was related to the author by Eva Wasson (now Eva Pancho) on the afternoon of May 7, 1944, a year after Annie's death.

[117] The number five had significance for the Paiutes, and occurs as often as do the numbers three, seven, and twelve in white cultures.

[118] Material on the Northern Paiute (also known as the Paviotso) is generally restricted to studies of local bands or particular aspects of their culture and stands badly in need of evaluation and coordination. Ruth Underhill's *The Northern Paiute Indians of California and Nevada*, U.S. Office of Education, Indian Affairs, (Lawrence, Kansas: Haskell Institute, 1941) will serve as a general, though elementary introduction. For more specific information, see Omer C. Stewart's "Culture Element Distributions: XIV, Northern Paiute," *Anthropological Records*, IV, No. 3 (1941), 361–466; Isabel T. Kelly, *Ethnography of the Surprise Valley Paiute*, "Publications in American Archaeology and Ethnology," XXXI, No. 3 (Berkeley: University of California Press, 1932), and "Northern Paiute Tales," *Journal of American Folklore*, LI, No. 202 (1938); Julian H. Steward, "Two Paiute Autobiographies," *Publications in American Archaeology and Ethnology*, XXXIII, No. 5 (Berkeley: University of California Press, 1934), 423–438; Robert H. Lowie, "Shoshonean Tales," *Journal of American Folklore*, XXXVII, Nos. 143–144 (1924), and *Notes on Shoshonean Ethnography*, "American Museum of Natural History Anthropological Papers," XX (1924), 193–294; Willard Z. Park, *Shamanism in Western North America*, "Publications in Social Sciences," No. 2 (Evanston, Illinois: Northwestern University, 1938), and "Paviotso Polyandry," *American Anthropologist*, XXXIX (1937), 366–368; Willard Z. Park, *et al.*, "Tribal Distribution in the Great Basin," *American Anthropologist*, XL, No. 4 (1938), 622–638; Margaret M. Wheat, *Notes on Paviotso Material Culture*, "Nevada State Museum Anthropological Pa-

pers," No. 1 (Carson City, Nevada: October, 1959); Robert F. Heizer, *Notes on Some Paviotso Personalities and Material Culture,* "Nevada State Museum Anthropological Papers," No. 2 (Carson City, Nevada: January, 1960). Also of interest is Sarah Winnemucca Hopkins, *Life Among the Paiutes; Their Wrongs and Claims* (Boston: Putnam's, 1883). However, much of the book's ethnological data is faulty, and should be re-evaluated in the light of modern scholarship. It should also be mentioned that Margaret Wheat is now preparing a profusely illustrated book for the University of Nevada Press, tentatively named *Lost Arts of the Primitive Paiutes.*

[119] Their marriage was never solemnized and consisted only in their cohabitation. Thus, by white standards the marriage was not binding, but in the eyes of the Indians it was entirely valid.

[120] O. C. Stewart, "Northern Paiute," p. 139.

[121] In 1936, Annie thought herself to be sixty-nine years old. Her obituary, printed in the *Review-Miner,* April 22, 1943, gives her date of birth as November 13, 1866. However, the census records of 1880 give Annie's age as seven years, which would make her date of birth approximately 1873. *United States Census, 1880* (Nevada, Humboldt County, Lake Township), p. 6.

BIBLIOGRAPHY

Angel, Myron, ed. *History of Nevada* (a reproduction of the Thompson and West edition of 1881), intro. David F. Myrick. Berkeley: Howell-North Books, 1958.

Bancroft, Hubert Howe. *History of Nevada, Colorado, and Wyoming.* San Francisco: A. L. Bancroft & Company, 1890.

Cline, Gloria Griffen. "Peter Skene Ogden's Nevada Explorations," *Nevada Historical Quarterly,* III, No. 3 (1960), 3–11.

―――. *Exploring the Great Basin.* Norman: University of Oklahoma Press, 1963.

Frémont, John C. *Report of the Exploring Expedition to the Rocky Mountains in the Year 1842, and to Oregon and North California in the Years 1843–44.* 28 Cong., 2 sess., House Exec. Doc. 166 (1845).

Geiger, Vincent, and Wakeman Bryarly. *Trail to California,* ed. D. M. Potter. New Haven: Yale University Press, 1945.

Heizer, Robert F., and Alex D. Kreiger. *Archaeology of Humboldt Cave, Churchill County, Nevada.* ("Publications in American Archaeology and Ethnology," XLVII, No. 1.) Berkeley: University of California Press, 1956.

Heizer, Robert F. *Executions by Stoning Among the Sierra Miwok and Northern Paiute.* ("Kroeber Anthropological Society Papers," No. 12.) Berkeley: 1955.

―――. *Notes on Some Paviotso Personalities and Material Culture.* ("Nevada State Museum Anthropological Papers," No. 2.) Carson City: January, 1960.

Hodge, Frederic Webb, (ed.). *Handbook of American Indians North of Mexico.* 2 vols. ("Bureau of American Ethnology Bulletin No. 30.") Washington, 1912.

Hopkins, Sarah Winnemucca. *Life Among the Paiutes; Their Wrongs and Claims,* ed. Mrs. Horace Mann. Boston: Putnam's, 1883.

Irving, Washington. *The Adventures of Captain Bonneville, U. S. A., in the Rocky Mountains and the Far West.* New York: G. P. Putnam's 1868.

Kelly, Isabel T. *Ethnography of the Surprise Valley Paiute.*("*Publications in Archaeology and Ethnology,*" XXXI, No. 3.) Berkeley: University of California Press, 1932.

——. "Northern Paiute Tales," *Journal of American Folklore,* LI, No. 202 (1938).

Leonard, Zenas. *Adventures of Zenas Leonard, Fur Trader,* ed. John C. Ewers. Norman: University of Oklahoma Press, 1959.

Loud, Llewellyn L., and M. R. Harrington. *Lovelock Cave.* ("Publications in American Archaeology and Ethnology," XXV, No. 1.) Berkeley: University of California Press, 1929.

Lowie, Robert H. "Shoshonean Tales," *Journal of American Folklore,* XXXVII, Nos. 143–144 (1924).

——. *Notes on Shoshonean Ethnography.* ("American Museum of Natural History Anthropological Papers." XX) New York, 1924, pp. 193–294.

Marcy, Randolph Barnes. *The Prairie Traveller.* New York: Harper & brothers, 1859.

Morgan, Dale L. *The Humboldt, Highroad of the West.* New York: Farrar and Rhinehart, 1943.

Myrick, David F. *Railroads of Nevada and Eastern California. I.* Berkeley: Howell-North Books, 1962-.

Nidever, George. *The Life and Adventures of George Nidever,* ed. William H. Ellison. Berkeley: University of California Press, 1937.

Ogden, Peter Skene. "The Peter Skene Ogden Journals; Snake Country Expedition, 1827–28 and 1828–29," ed. T. C. Elliott, *Oregon Historical Society Quarterly,* XI (December, 1910), 355-99.

Park, Willard Z. "Paviotso Polyandry." *American Anthropologist,* XXXIX (1937), 366–368.

——. *Shamanism in Western North America.* ("Publications in Social Sciences," No. 2.) Evanston, Illinois: Northwestern University, 1938.

Park, Willard Z., et al. "Tribal Distribution in the Great Basin." *American Anthropologist,* XL, No. 4 (1938), 622–38.

Preuss, Charles. *Exploring With Frémont.* Trans. and ed. Erwin G. and Elizabeth K. Gudde. Norman: University of Oklahoma Press, 1958.

Reed, Mabel L. "History of the Development of Lovelock Valley," unpublished B. A. thesis, University of Nevada, 1909.

Roe, Frank G. *The Indian and the Horse.* Norman: University of Oklahoma Press, 1955.

Scott, Kenneth D. *Frozen Grass.* New York: Carlton Press, 1960.

Smith, Philip Dodd, Jr. "Sagebrush Soldiers: Nevada's Volunteers in the Civil War." *Nevada Historical Society Quarterly,* V, Nos. 3–4 (1962).

Steward, Julian H. "Native Cultures of the Intermontane (Great Basin) Area," in *Essays in Historical Anthropology,* pp. 445–502. Washington, D.C.: The Smithsonian Institute, 1940.

————. *Two Paiute Autobiographies.* ("Publications in American Archaeology and Ethnology," XXXIII, No. 5.) Berkeley: University of California Press, 1934, pp. 423–438.

Stewart, George R. *The California Trail.* New York: McGraw-Hill, 1962.

Stewart, Omer C. "Northern Paiute Bands." *Anthropological Records,* II, No. 3 (1939), 127–149.

————. "Culture Element Distributions: XIV, Northern Paiute." *Anthropological Records,* IV, No. 3 (1941), 361–446.

Thompson and West. *History of Nevada,* see under Angel.

Underhill, Ruth. *The Northern Paiute Indians of California and Nevada,* U.S. Office of Education, Indian Affairs. Lawrence, Kansas: Haskell Institute, 1941.

United States Census Office, "9th Census, Nevada, 1870"; *and* "10th Census, Nevada, 1880." Microfilm, University of Nevada Library.

Wheat, Margaret M. *Notes on Paviotso Material Culture.* ("Nevada State Museum Anthropological Papers," No. 1.) Carson City: October, 1959.

Wren, Thomas. *A History of the State of Nevada.* New York: Lewis Publishing Company, 1904.

Wright, William. *The Big Bonanza,* intro. Oscar Lewis. New York: A. A. Knopf, 1959.

CPSIA information can be obtained
at www.ICGtesting.com
Printed in the USA
LVHW031928060323
741034LV00004B/317

9 781664 274648